CULTURE SHOCK !

Turkey

Arın Bayraktaroğlu

Graphic Arts Center Publishing Company
Portland, Oregon

In the same series

Australia	Ireland	South Africa	A Globe-Trotter's Guide
Borneo	Israel	Spain	A Student's Guide
Britain	Italy	Sri Lanka	A Traveller's Medical Guide
Burma	Japan	Switzerland	A Wife's Guide
Canada	Korea	Syria	Working Holidays Abroad
China	Malaysia	Taiwan	
Denmark	Morocco	Thailand	
France	Nepal	USA	
Germany	Norway	USA—The South	
Hong Kong	Pakistan	Vietnam	
India	Philippines		
Indonesia	Singapore		

Illustrations by Tan Oral

© 1996 Times Editions Pte Ltd

This book is published by special
arrangement with Times Editions Pte Ltd
Times Centre, 1 New Industrial Road, Singapore 536196
International Standard Book Number 1-55868-253-8
Graphic Arts Center Publishing Company
P.O. Box 10306 • Portland, Oregon 97210 • (503) 226-2402

Printed in Singapore

To Kerem, his father and his grandfather.

CONTENTS

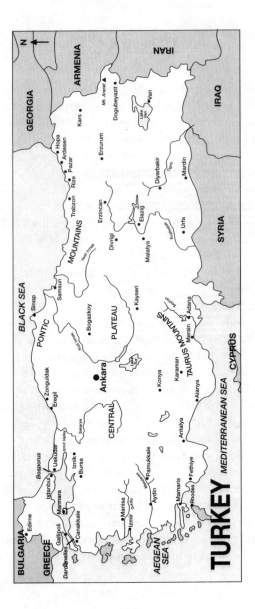

PREFACE

When Turks meet friends in unexpected, remote locations they say, "The world is small." The saying has never been closer to the truth than at present times because, thanks to the advances in technology, the world is right in their sitting room every night. But while the Turks educate themselves as to the peculiarities of most nations, cultures and lands, they still remain something of a mystery to the rest of the world, surrounded by a hazy cloud called the Orient. Turkish delight, carpets, towels, cigarettes and coffee are all that most outsiders can associate with the country, yet beyond this parsimonious list one of the richest of cultures and the most welcoming of hosts lies, waiting to be discovered and appreciated.

In an age when most holiday albums burst with photographs of the same Mediterranean spots and therefore are no longer personal and attractive, Turkey is rapidly becoming the darling of innovative holiday makers. Those who come to sample its riches do not regret their choice either because there is a lot on offer here: Mount Ararat and Lake Van in the east; the ancient cities of Troy, Ephesus and Aphrodisias (its name taken from the goddess of love) in the west; Sumela Monastery in Trabzon, magnanimously built on sheer cliffs in the north, and in the south, the golden beaches where Cleopatra is said to have watched the sunset, to name but a few. Turkey's scenic wonders extend to such inland treasures as Pamukkale, the cascading limestone pools and rivulets forming an indescribable tower of cotton-whiteness with crystal blue water resting in the pools, monumental statues on Mount Nemrut and the fairy-chimneys of once-volcanic Cappadocia. Of course, there is also the jewel in the crown, Istanbul, they city of slender minarets, ancient churches, beautiful palaces and exquisite foundations (not forgetting 20th century additions like the slums and squatters quarters).

While all this and many more attractions fill the pages of the travel books on the shelves marked "Turkey" in the bookshops, the culture as well as the people with their customs, character and mannerisms remain largely unknown. For today's visitors, knowing, for example, how to communicate with the Turks, how to please them or avoid conflict, how to join in their merriment or be respectful on sensitive issues is more important than simply learning the history of this amphitheatre or the whereabouts of that ancient site.

This knowledge is even more essential for business entrepreneurs (expected to increase in numbers now that Turkey has joined the European Customs Union), academics, researchers, cultural enthusiasts or simply retired people in search of a gentle climate, all of whom want to feel at ease in the country, whether temporarily or on a permanent basis.

This book is prepared with such priorities and needs in mind. Rub the magic lamp and enter the cave. You will meet in this unknown land so many new friends that you will agree, it is a small world, after all.

Chapter One

INTRODUCING TURKEY

GEOGRAPHY

Turkey is situated in the northern hemisphere at an equal distance from the equator and the North Pole and at the junction of Europe and Asia. It is roughly rectangular in shape, and the surface area of the country is 814,578 square kilometres (505,038 square miles). Most of its territory is in Asia, although a fraction takes in European soil. Despite the fact that it is surrounded by sea on three sides (the Black Sea in the north, the Aegean in the west and the Mediterranean in the south), it has enough inland borders to separate it from as many as seven neighbours – two on the European side; Greece and Bulgaria and five on the Asian, namely; Georgia, Armenia, Iran, Iraq and Syria. The Black Sea joins the Aegean and henceforth the Mediterranean through the Sea of Marmara, and the straits of the Dardanelles and the Bosporus.

Anatolia, as the Asian soil is otherwise known (yet another name given to it is Asia Minor), is a high plateau rising gradually towards the east with a number of river valleys snaking across the landscape. Among these, the most well known belong to the famous biblical Dicle (Tigris) and Fırat (Euphrates). These two rivers cross the border into Iraq, where they merge, but the others flow into the sea around Turkey. The longest river, however, is the Kızıl Irmak, which flows into the Black Sea, after making a large curve in the heart of Anatolia.

The mountains in the north and south run parallel to the sea and the coastline on both sides is less indented and protracted than the Aegean. Within the plateau there are lake districts too, most notably in the western part of the Taurus mountains and around the Sea of Marmara. The largest of Turkey's lakes, Lake Van, lies in the east near Mount Ararat and the two together create one of the most picturesque and dreamlike scenes in the world.

Ankara, traditionally famous for its Angora goats – hence angora wool – is the capital of modern Turkey but in terms of cultural, social and economic affairs the country's heart still beats in the old metropolis, Istanbul. These two, as well as Izmir on the Aegean coast, Adana and Antalya on the Mediterranean, and Eskisehir and Bursa in central Anatolia, are the major points of concentration for a sizeable portion of the population, which is nearing 60 million. Migration to big cities started in the 1950s due to socio-economic problems and accelerated in the period 1985–95, when people in the underdeveloped southeast region started moving to the urban areas in the west to escape the problems created by unemployment and the underdevelopment of the region. This not only failed to solve one set of problems but created others in and around the large cities. Once the Atatürk Dam (which will be one of the ten largest dams in the world) and the gigantic G.A.P. (Southeast Anatolian Project) are completed, it is expected that the benefits will be so far-reaching that the opportunities they provide will encourage people to move back to their original homelands.

CLIMATE

The diversity in the landscape results in different climatic conditions throughout the country. In central Anatolia a Continental climate prevails, with hot summers, cold winters, and limited rainfall. The coastline in the south and the west gets hot in the summer but enjoys mild winters with occasional outbreaks of rain. The north has a moderate climate in all seasons but the weather in the east is harsh, with the winter temperature dropping as low as –35°C. In contrast, the southeast is unbearably hot, with temperatures reaching 45°C at the peak of the summer season, creating a perfect habitat for snakes and scorpions. The regional temperatures (in centigrade) average as follows:

Mediterranean	17.2
East Anatolia	8.1
Aegean	14.3
South East Anatolia	16.0
Central Anatolia	10.7
Black Sea	12.5
Marmara	14.2

In most cities, but especially in Istanbul, people suffer from high air pollution in winter. This is because low-grade charcoal or lignite is used as the main source of energy for heating. Work to bring natural gas to Istanbul is under way but until it is completed people will seek a remedy in wearing gas masks in the open air.

HISTORY

The world's first town, a neolithic city at Çatalhöyük, dates back to 6,500 BC. Since then many civilisations, namely those of the Hattis, Hittites, Phrygians, Unartians, Lycians, Lydians, Ionians, Persians, Macedonians, Romans and Byzantines have flourished in Anatolia, each leaving its mark on the landscape with ancient sites and ruins, and contributing to the progress of modern civilisation.

The ruins of Hadrian's Temple in Ephesus – evidence of the Roman Empire's influence in ancient Turkey. (Photo: Turkish Tourist Office)

The Turks themselves started coming from the steppes of Central Asia as early as the 11th century. They established the Anatolian Seljuk State in the 12th century. They had adopted the Mohammedan faith from the 10th century onwards. The name Ottoman, which came to be used for the Turks later on, originates from the name of Sultan Osman, the founder and first ruler of the Ottoman principality. In 1453 Sultan Mehmet II (1451–81) conquered Constantinople (later to be called Istanbul), which became the capital of the Ottoman state. From then on, and for the next two hundred years, there was no stopping the Turks. They expanded in all directions and formed one of the largest empires of all time, especially during the reign of Sultan Suleiman often known as Suleiman the Magnificent (1520–66).

At this time the lands they ruled stretched from East Anatolia to the outskirts of Vienna, from the Crimea to North Africa and some parts of the Arabian Peninsula, including the holy cities of Mecca and Medina. With the conquest of Mecca, the Caliphate (the title once used by the descendants of the Prophet Mohammed) passed to the Ottoman sultans. The first major setback for the Ottomans was experienced in the siege of Vienna in the last quarter of the 17th century. Other defeats followed, until in the 19th century "The Sick Man of Europe," as the Czar of Russia, Nicholas I had christened the Turkish realm, decided to shake off its misfortunes by a series of reform movements and by Westernising its institutions. However, the country later made the mistake of going into the First World War on the side of the Central Powers, thus emerging from it defeated and in the hands of occupying forces. Even the Greeks, over whom the Empire ruled for more than 400 years, came to Anatolia to claim some territory. On the verge of a final collapse in 1922 a young general named Mustafa Kemal started the War of Independence, rid the country of its foreign invaders, and a new state rose out of the ashes of the old Empire.

The Dolmabahce Palace Gate – an archtectural reminder of Turkey's rich history. (Photo: Turkish Tourist Office)

15

MUSTAFA KEMAL "ATATÜRK"

Mustafa Kemal was a soldier by profession but the depth of vision and courage he embodied is rarely found even in experienced statesmen. After organising and then monitoring the War of Independence, he set up a new parliament in Ankara in 1923, proclaimed the state to be a republic and was elected the first president. As he died in 1938, his presidency lasted for only fifteen years but within this short period of time he managed to transform his country to such an extent that even his immediate predecessors would not have recognised it.

To start with, the administrative, legal, and educational systems were changed. The constitution was rewritten. The state became secular and populist. The Caliphate was abolished and so were the religious orders. The script was changed by replacing the Arabic alphabet with the Latin one and the language was purged of foreign elements. Polygamy was prohibited and international time and the international calendar were adopted. Women were given the right to vote and be voted for. The old fez was cast out and the European hat was brought in.

When the new law of surnames passed through the parliament, the nation gave Mustafa Kemal the name *Atatürk*, (Father of the Turks). Indeed, the adoration he has inspired amongst his fellow countrymen falls only a little short of the love of God. Today, any office you enter will have his picture on the wall, and if you happen to be in Turkey on November 10, the date of his death, you will see the whole country come to a standstill at 9:05 a.m. for five minutes. Turks will stop literally wherever they are to mourn Atatürk, be it on the way to work, ascending a flight of stairs, or halfway through a bowl of lentil soup!

POLITICS AND POLITICAL PARTIES

For the first twenty-two years of the republic, Turkey had a parliamentary system but it was ruled by one party, The Republican People's Party, alone. A multi-party political system arrived in 1946 with the foundation of The Democrat Party which, as is generally the case after long term autocratic rule, swept into power in 1950 with a landslide victory.

The Republican People's Party was in favour of state monopolies and had statist and interventionist programmes, while the new Democrat Party was supportive of the private sector and free enterprise. In the next ten years the country was treated as the rope in a tug-of-war between these two political views. The animosity reached such heights, that in 1960 the army stepped in to topple The Democrat Party on the pretext of restoring social order. The country returned to parliamentary rule again in 1961 but only to have the right-wing views of The Democrat Party carried forward under a different name – The Justice Party. In the meantime another party, The Nationalist Movement Party, was becoming prominent because its nationalistic and pan-Turkish views were seen by some as a barrier to militant left-wingers. The following twenty years saw the friction between the right and the left escalating and turning into serious armed confrontations.

Amidst this confusion, a new voice started to be heard, that of the religious factions, which had been suppressed until then. This voice became incarnate in The National Order Party. When the army stepped in again in 1980, the situation was just short of civil war. Power was given to the civilians in 1983 but the intervention had succeeded in creating discontinuity amongst party members. The right-wingers gathered under two different banners: The Motherland Party and The True Path Party. The social democrats had also divided into several parties. The Nationalist Movement Party (pan-Turkish) gained strength once more after the disintegration of the Russian Federation and the emergence of the Turkic states in Central Asia. While the old enmities between the right and left continued, the benefits of their fragmentation were reaped by the new religious group, The Welfare Party, which was founded after the coup of 1980 and which in the 1994 municipality elections secured 28% of the votes, finishing the race as the front runner.

The enthusiasm for division shows no sign of abating. On the contrary, the number of parties contending for the popular vote is on the increase. As a result, the country has had three coalition governments in four years. This pattern of unlikely coalitions looks set to continue following the December 1995 poll, which saw The Welfare Party again secure the most votes but the other parties scrambling to form partnerships to take power. Unless some of these parties unite around the common denominators, it is wishful thinking to imagine that Turkey can have a single-party government in the years to come.

ADMINISTRATION

The president is the head of state, representing the republic and national unity. After each election, he invites the leader of the political party which has won the majority of the seats in the National Assembly to be prime minister. The prime minister in turn, elects the members of the Council of Ministers.

On the local scale, the administration is in the hands of provincial governments, the heads of which (the governors) are the link between the area and the central government. The municipalities, on the other hand, are autonomous and responsible for the public amenities such as electricity, gas, water and public transport.

Public law and order is maintained by the police force and the semi-military Gendarmerie Organisation. There is also the Coast Guard Organisation, undertaking the administration of the coasts.

The power of the judiciary is exercised by judicial, military and administrative courts. After these courts pronounce their verdict, it goes to the superior courts for approval and a final ruling.

ECONOMY

In the early years of the republic, the private sector was not developed enough to be a locomotive to the economy so the state had to make substantial investments. This is how the state came to own factories and manufacturing compounds. At the time, this was acceptable but nowadays people feel that the state owns too many commodities, from sugar to cement, from textiles to cigarettes. Since the 1920s a lot of changes have taken place in Turkey. The private sector is now involved in industry, science, technology, telecommunications and transportation. Today, Turkey even produces some armaments for the use of its armed forces. The conditions are ripe for a common market economy to flourish, so for the last decade or so, the governments in power have been trying to prepare the social and economic conditions for the privatisation of state-owned facilities. Once this is achieved, the state will be able to spare more funds, enabling it to concentrate on its social and administrative services.

Another ill to be remedied if a strong economy is to be achieved is the just and adequate collection of taxes from everybody. At present

The Afsin-Elbistan power project to utilise low calorie lignite coal – part of the developing infrastructure underpinning Turkey's development. (Photo: Turkish Tourist Office)

19

there are more people who manage to avoid paying their taxes than there are people who are taxed. This is because Turkey has a high proportion of self-employed people and no efficient system for tracking them down. What is more, those who are taxed, for example the civil servants and the workers, fall into the low-paid category and taxing them does not bring high revenues to the government anyway. Additionally, the fact that people with low salaries are paying taxes while the high earners are not paying at all or paying less than their share is creating serious cracks in the social foundation.

Today tourism contributes considerably to the Turkish economy. On the trade side, textiles are the number one export item followed by agricultural products, the main crops being wheat, cotton, tea, rice, tobacco, hazelnuts and fruit. Turkey was accepted into the European Customs Union on January 1, 1996 and the economic effects of this are keenly anticipated.

THE ARMY

According to the constitution, military service is required of every Turkish man, so all male citizens enlist as soon as they reach the age of 20, unless they have a good reason for not doing so, such as a physical or psychological impediment or still being in education.

Turkey is a member of NATO and has the second largest army among the member countries. (The largest is that of the United States.) Military service lasts for 18 months and most men consider it a national duty and accept it when the time comes. Those who find ways to delay it unnecessarily face difficulties in getting permanent jobs or even a wife, as the general view is that a man does not settle down until he has done his military service. There may also be other advantages in doing it sooner rather than later – the literacy courses and technological training given during service turn some conscripts into qualified personnel with better job prospects in civilian life.

The mission of the army is defined as protection of the land against internal as well as external threats. With this double responsibility, the army has to be watchful over many fronts. Apart from the fact that Turkey is geographically located in an area with severe international conflicts, there are also the internal problems related to politics and differing ethnic origins.

Recently, the army was saddled with the further responsibility of being a peacemaker when there were clashes between the police and people in Gaziosmanpasa (the Alevi district of Istanbul) and it was called in to pacify the situation. It may be the sword of Damocles over Turkish democracy but people expect, and in some cases encourage, the generals to step in if the politicians fail to provide solutions. A famous journalist and television commentator, Güneri Cıvaoglu, once said in his program that in times of trouble, journalists would go and watch the windows of the Chief of the General Staff's room at night: if they were dark, those standing outside could all go home and sleep peacefully, but if the lights were switched on, they would alert their newspapers to the next day's coup d'état.

RELIGION

Despite the fact that Turkey guarantees freedom of worship to non-Muslims, 98% of the Turkish population is Muslim. The constitution also declares that the state is based on the principle of secularism, i.e. not interfering in the creeds and beliefs of its citizens. However, in recent years the members of the Alevi minority, who hold very liberal views within the Muslim sects, have started voicing complaints about the fact that all religious education and facilities are biased towards the Sunni majority.

For the majority of people, religion is an issue between the individual and God and therefore the state should have no say in religious matters. The fact that the pro-Islamic Welfare Party came out of the 1995 general elections as the biggest party alarmed many Westerners who thought that this was another case of fundamentalism taking over a country. Turkish political analysts, however, have a different view and point out that the Welfare Party in fact received

21

only 20% of the vote while 80% was divided up between the secularist parties, hardly a result to indicate that fundamentalism is gaining hold in Turkey. A lot of the support for the Welfare Party is also attributed to protest votes against the disappointing performance of the parties on the left.

All educated Turks I talked to about this change gave me more or less the same interpretation. They claim that migration to industrialised centres brought people who had, until then, led a very closed village life, face to face with riches and luxuries that they did not know existed. It was quite natural that they suffered a culture shock and a feeling of alienation as a result of this. Religion was the only force within their grasp that offered them security in an estranged environment. The situation for the next generation, however, will likely be different. They will be born into and brought up within the urban culture and will develop a natural immunity to it right from the start.

Chapter Two

THE TURKS

EAST OR WEST, HOME IS BEST

Despite their central Asian origins and having Islam as their religion, for the last 200 years the Turks have been trying to modernise their country on the model of Western Europe. During the Ottoman period such reforms were confined to military matters but after the foundation of the republic the changes were brought into other areas too. The civil and penal codes were changed so as to be in line with those in Switzerland and education was secularised, as in France. Although the traditional fez was abolished and replaced with a European hat by a decree, there was no such legal pressure on any other clothes or furniture but both changed rapidly, as European fashion dictated. Today the Turks consider themselves both Eastern and Western, a mixture of both, symbolically like their country, which is partly in Europe and partly in Asia.

The Turkish art historian, Gülru Necipoglu, of Harvard University claims in her book, *The Topkapi Palace in the Fifteenth and Sixteenth Centuries,* that the synthesis is due to the expansionary policies of the Ottoman Turks. The place where the Topkapi Palace (made famous by the film of the same name) was built in Istanbul is the very point where the two continents (Asia and Europe) and two seas (the Black Sea and the Sea of Marmara) meet. Similarly, at the entrance of the palace, the portal inscription describes Mehmet the Conqueror (of Constantinople) as, "The Sultan of the two continents and two seas" (Berreyn and Bahreyn Padisahı).

Presently the Turks have no such claims but have retained their unique character embodying this duality. The combination is not an

The old and the new sit comfortably alongside each other in Turkey. (Photo: Turkish Tourist Office)

easy one and there are those who advocate that the country should go in one direction only, so that it might have a clearer national identity. Most Turks, however, are content with their present situation, they think that it enriches their life and culture. In almost all urban homes there are two types of toilet; one, the western pedestal, and the other, oriental, with two raised platforms for the feet and a hole. The shopping areas are full of shops with the western brand names alongside the Turkish ones. In a shop window one may see a set of Myson crockery sitting next to a wall plate with an Arabic inscription on it. One of the two bridges over the Bosporus was built by an English-German consortium, while the contract for the other went to the Japanese. It was similarly interesting that just before the agreement for Turkey to be accepted into the European Customs Union was signed in Brussels in 1995, the prime minister, Tansu Ciller, visited Japan for the first time to increase business relations with this country. It is as if Turkey feels it should counterbalance each move taken towards the West with one in the opposite direction.

Some pro-Europeans impatiently say that Turkey is like a passenger running west on the deck of a ship going to the east. The truth is that it is going west but in the footsteps of the old Ottoman Janisseries – three steps forward, followed by one backwards.

CITY VERSUS VILLAGE

In all countries the villagers or rural populations are different from the urban dwellers, but in few countries is the difference between the two as striking as it has been in Turkey. In the past, this difference applied to everything from appearances to behaviour but since the communications revolution, which has affected Turkey as much as it has other parts of the world, the gap has been narrowing.

I remember a very colourful and conspicuous distant relative of mine from Istanbul recounting an experience she had on the outskirts of Erzurum, a less developed region in the east of Turkey. The year was 1961. While her husband was in the area making a civil service

25

Traditional methods still prevail in many Turkish villages as this scene of Cotton-field workers shows. (Photo: Turkish Tourist Office)

inspection, she decided to take a walk on her own in the lonely streets near her hotel. As usual she was dressed and made up in a way that would have turned heads even in relatively tolerant Istanbul: a miniskirt, a colourful, long necklace of beads, and a hat with pink and white flowers. As she was walking down a street, she saw a black object approaching her. What could it be? The thing got closer and when there was only an arms length between the two, my relative realised that it was a local woman, dressed in a huge black cloth, covering her from head to toe. Even her face was hidden behind this cover, leaving only a slit where her eyes were supposed to be – and the eyes gazing through this gap were filled with astonishment as they travelled from the flowery hat down to the naked legs. The two stopped and stared at each other for a few minutes, as if they were creatures from different planets, rather than women of the same country, and then each went on her own way. My relative later asked me, "How can a woman dress like this?" No doubt, the other person was asking her relatives the same question.

Like those in many other countries, the village people in Turkey are conservative, less educated, naive and direct, while the city people are complicated, sophisticated, adaptable and educated. These are the features respectively found in Karagöz and Hacivat, the two main characters of the famous Turkish shadow theatre which was the only source of entertainment both in the urban and rural areas from the 16th century down to the 1950s. Karagöz, as the shadow theatre is otherwise referred to, is a blunt, straightforward, bold and uneducated character who is prone to accidents and makes a lot of social and linguistic gaffes. He is the personification of the village man. Hacivat, on the other hand, is better educated, shrewd and sophisticated, and patronises Karagöz whenever he makes a mistake. Compared to the popular couples of other cultures such as Punch and Judy or Laurel and Hardy, Karagöz and Hacivat are important not merely as sources of fun but as personifications of real character types that have lived in the area for many centuries, and this accounts for their popularity.

Today, because of good communication systems, increased distribution of newspapers, local and national radio stations and private television channels, rural Turkey is not as impenetrable as it used to be, so you are less likely to bump into people as naive as Karagöz. With a large number of rural dwellers moving to big cities and forming shanty towns around them, these days everybody is a Hacivat, to some degree – a sad but inevitable situation in an age tending to globalisation.

CHARACTERISTICS

Whether from a rural or urban background most Turks have certain characteristics in common. It is on the grounds of this mixture that one can talk about what differentiates a Turk from other nationals. Some of these characteristics are listed on the following pages.

Patriotism

To start with, Turks are extremely patriotic. The first thing every child does at school in the morning is to chant: "I am a Turk, I am correct and hard-working. I am ready to sacrifice my existence for the existence of Turkey."

These patriotic feelings can be easily aroused – a feature which is an asset provided that they are regulated by clever leaders, as was the case in the War of Independence. However, they may also lead to comical situations if aroused too quickly. In the late sixties when the stories of hardships suffered by the Cypriot Turks at the hands of their Greek compatriots had been reaching mainland Turkey, there was an open air meeting in Mersin, a southern port. Apparently the speaker, having made several references to these unfortunate events, concluded his speech by saying, "Come on brothers, let us go and put a stop to this nonsense!" No sooner had it been said, than a group from the excited audience dived into the sea and started swimming in the direction of the island, about 64 kilometres away. After half an hour's struggle with the gigantic waves, the swimmers realised that Cyprus was not as near as its lights at night had suggested, and all returned to shore, their mission unaccomplished.

The country and its symbol, the flag, are of prime importance. The Turkish national anthem opens with the lines: "Don't despair, until the last stove in this country is extinguished, this red flag will fly in the sky." Having such a respect for their own flag, they have difficulty in understanding how some other nationals can make carrier bags, lighters, ashtrays, T-shirts and even shorts and underpants decorated with the pattern of their flags.

The Turk – Philanthropist and Lover

The Turks have a romantic nature. They can fall in love at first sight and propose marriage at the second meeting. They like melancholic attachments too. Most of their songs and poems are about unfulfilled, unrequited love. They give easily, whether of their affections or worldly goods. A complete stranger sitting next to you on a bus or a train may offer you half of his modest ration, wrapped up in newspaper. "I like you" *(seni sevdim)* is a common type of evaluation that a first time encounter usually finishes with, unless you do something really drastic to prevent it.

To Be Or Not To Be Angry

The Turks usually put on a serious face. Especially in official contexts, transactions are carried out in the utmost solemnity, which some may find discouraging. It has to be appreciated, however, that seriousness is associated with the truth and when there is a need to underline the actuality of something the Turks are dead serious. In official contexts seriousness is the expected demeanour and creates confidence in the transaction.

Some foreigners who have been to Turkey would describe the Turks as quick-tempered and hot-headed. This is because one minute peace may prevail and the next, voices and fists may be raised for no apparent reason. It is true that some individuals are quick to adopt a warlike posture, but reason, of course, is a relative matter and what does not seem to be a good cause in one culture may be extremely offensive in another.

Luckily, they forgive and forget easily too. In fact, given their quick-tempered nature, it is surprising how tolerant they can be in situations which may be intolerable in most other cultures. More often than not, they interpret things positively. Even a clock which is out of action will at least show the correct time twice a day, they say.

Pride and Prejudice

The Turks are an individualistic people who find it difficult to work as a team. They are too competitive for that. They like to be appreciated and any hint of ridicule creates offence. If two of them get together in your presence, you will note that the conversation is conducted mainly in Turkish even if they can both speak English. When this happens, do not get paranoid, they are not talking about or against you, it is just that they are avoiding giving one another the chance to laugh at the mistakes they might make in English.

Ne Bakıyorsun? – What Are You Looking At?

The Turks love looking at people and do not understand how most Europeans can manage to ignore one another by fixing their eyes only on the advertisement panels while travelling in crowded underground carriages. They look when they like you, when they find you different or eccentric, or when they think you are abhorrent. Which of these has prompted the look may not be obvious to strangers to the culture, but they themselves are trained enough to understand the distinction.

It is not bad to be gazed at as an object of admiration, but gawping provokes a snappy reaction: "What are you looking at?" which can be extended into more complicated and adverse structures: "What are you looking at? Haven't you seen a human being before?" or; "What are you looking at like a cow watching a train in motion?" I was once on a beach in Antalya in the days when topless tourists were a novelty to the area. Members of a Turkish family were on sun beds placed next to mine. The husband and wife were oblivious to the environment but their young son was looking at the topless bodies around him so intently that his mother felt the need to warn him herself and said,

"What are you looking at, haven't you seen naked women before?" The poor little boy responded naively, "No, I haven't." Being only four or five, he was indeed young enough to be having the experience for the first time in his life.

SEXUAL MATTERS

Sexual matters may be puzzling for a stranger in Turkey. There are not many cuddling couples out in the open to suggest that this is a permissive society but the national newspapers are full of photographs which belie this. Similarly confusing are the advertisements for the 0900 numbers on some private television channels, broadcast after midnight. The truth is that sex has different meanings for men and women. The culture does not repress men in terms of their sexuality; on the contrary it encourages them and men often talk about their sexual experiences, even if half of them are figments of their imagination.

In contrast, the female who is concerned about her reputation should show no hint of an interest in sexuality. Chastity is still important and brides are expected to be virgins. This is why one does not see many girls holding hands with, let alone kissing, a boyfriend in public. Things are changing quickly, however, although areas where boyfriends and girlfriends can go and be alone are quite restricted. Some of their favourite haunts are the upper floors of fast-food restaurants. Foreign visitors go to such places for a quick snack between bouts of shopping, but young Turks often see them as refuges from parental eyes.

Does this encouragement to men and discouragement to women not create problems? Of course it does. It creates a continuous cat-and-mouse chase. While the woman is always on the run, the man will follow her with innuendos, wolf-whistles her, and calls her a "peanut" (not a single peanut in its oval shape but the two of them in their shell, which is similar in shape to an hourglass). Turkish women are so used to this that outside Turkey they can feel depressed over the lack of

31

attention. One who settled down in Germany said, "In the first couple of years of my life outside Turkey I lived with an inferiority complex in the belief that no one found me attractive any more."

Men Versus Women

Following from the above, there are different behaviour patterns expected from and exhibited by men and women. As perhaps in no other culture, the best examples of either sex are defined by the emphasis placed on their sex: a 'womanly woman' *(hanım hanımcık kadın)* and a 'manly man' *(erkek adam)*.

A 'womanly woman' is quiet, shy, fearful, yet a good housewife. She may or may not wear a headscarf but suggestive, sexy clothes are definitely out of the question. Her place is at home both before and after marriage. A 'manly man' is one who is brave, loud, virile, does not hesitate to fight for what he believes in, does not show his emotions or cry, and knows no fear. He usually has a moustache, and drinks and smokes a lot.

As more women have been opting for higher education in the last couple of decades, women these days are displaying fewer symptoms of being 'womanly women,' the benefits and drawbacks of which are openly discussed. A piece of graffiti was reported once in the entertainment section of a newspaper, with a comment saying that it was taken from the top of a desk in a university: "Good girls go to Paradise, but bad girls go anywhere they like."

However, the 'manly man' still has a strong hold on society. A modern, educated Turkish man recounted the following story. Apparently he had to travel from Eskisehir, a city in the middle of Anatolia, to Istanbul where he had urgent business to attend to. When he arrived at the airport he was told that the scheduled flight had been cancelled due to a lack of passengers and they were not going to mobilise the flight for just one passenger. While my friend was wringing his hands in frustration, an official from the nearby flying school approached him and asked whether he would like to go with them on an 'experimental flight.' The plane he offered was very small but my friend, who had no other alternative, accepted with alacrity, without giving any thought to the word 'experimental.' Once he was in his seat, however, he realised that the pilot in charge was a young trainee, being instructed by a tutor at his side about what he should and should not do. After a bumpy start my friend wished he had not accepted the offer so readily. He later said to me, "I wanted to tell them to stop and let me out there and then, but it was not a manly thing to do, so I shut up, closed my eyes and prayed for a safe journey all the way to Istanbul."

Görücü

Turkish society has inherited from the Ottoman times a premarital ceremony. In the old days, when the womenfolk did not go out of their homes without a cover on their face and did not mix with the men visiting their house, unmarried boys and girls had no context in which they could meet. The marriages then were formed on the recommendation of someone close to the boy's family about a certain girl with a good reputation. If it had created sufficient interest, a couple of women from the boy's side would pay a prearranged visit to the girl's house. The girl would offer water or Turkish coffee to the visitors while they accomplished their task of seeing her. This occasion, therefore, is rightly called, "the act of seeing" *(görücülük)* and the visitors, "the ones who see" *(görücü)*.

One might wonder whether seeing a girl just for a couple of minutes would be enough to decide about an important matter such as marriage. In the past, apparently there were some yardsticks used for this purpose. Those who are old enough recount stories from the Ottoman times about how some people looked at the girl's bed to see if it was properly made, and some asked her to cook rice which, once cooked, they threw at the wall in handfuls. If the chunks stuck on the wall, it meant that the girl had lost her chances of marrying this would-be suitor (good Turkish rice should not be sticky). Whether or not these were true, today such tests are unthinkable and people are content to base their judgement on the coffee offered to them.

In modern times most boys and girls find their own spouses but the old system has not been abandoned completely. Even when a boy and a girl meet outside their family circles and decide to get married, their families should get together before marriage so that the parents of the boy can formally ask for the hand of the girl and her parents can formally give their blessing to the union.

There are still visitors coming to see a girl who is a complete stranger to the young man in question. What happens when the girl is not interested in him? "There are ways to disenchant the visitors without being impolite," said a modern Istanbul girl. "I may be absent-minded and put salt in the coffee instead of sugar, or I may be too clumsy and spill the coffee on their clothes. The choice depends on how I feel on the day."

THE HOUSEHOLD

The Ottoman household was very crowded indeed. Not only did the sons stay at home after marriage, it was also the case that a man was allowed to have up to four wives.

With the coming of the Turkish Republic in 1924 all this was changed. Now it is one wife only. Furthermore, newly married couples start their own home rather than living with the boy's parents. Despite the changed system, some households are still crowded, but this time with children who, regardless of sex and age stay in the parental home until marriage. Turkey has got one of the highest birth rates in the world too. Especially in Eastern Anatolia, families with as many as seven to ten children are common and 60% of the whole population is said to be under 20 years of age.

MARRIAGE

Mothers start putting aside items for the trousseau almost as soon as the birth of their daughter. Bed linen, kitchen and bathroom towels, table cloths, pretty napkins and underwear accumulate to a hefty high by the time the girl reaches 17. For the sons, the fathers save a little each month so that when the time comes they will have enough to throw a marriage party which everybody can talk about. They also buy the bulk of the furniture for the new couple. It is customary that the girl's side provide for the bedroom and kitchen, while the boy's family is responsible for the contents of the sitting and dining rooms.

Although regional variations exist, the bridal gown is white as in the West and, until registration is complete, the bride wears her veil over her face. Only after the marriage vows are taken can the groom raise it and kiss her on the cheeks. In the old days when the marriages were arranged, this was the first time a man saw the face of his bride, sometimes to his horror. Nowadays this part of the ceremony is kept only as a ritual.

It is believed that whoever steps on the foot of the other during the registration ceremony will have the upper hand during the marriage, so most couples are too occupied with finding the foot of the other under the table to concentrate on what is happening above the table, but if they should forget about this, their friends will shout their heads off to remind them not to surrender so easily.

In some regions the tradition of pinning a bank-note on the bridal gown is retained but in urban weddings the gift is an item with practical use in the newly established home. People bring their presents to the couple on their first visit after the wedding. In the first few months after marriage, the newlyweds entertain day in and day out, to accept the presents. Bric-a-brac and kitchen or table wear are the most common items for a wedding gift but these days couples keep a list of the things they need, so asking for it in advance will avoid unnecessary time and worry.

DIVISION OF LABOUR WITHIN THE HOUSE

No matter who stepped on whose foot during the wedding ceremony, the house is definitely the wife's territory, and she rules with absolute authority.

To the Turkish woman, her home is more than her castle, it is her life and anything falling outside its boundaries, even her profession if she has one, is peripheral and instrumental. Of course, there are exceptions but they do not obliterate the rule. Within this setup, the husband has an almost lodger-like existence. Indeed, a husband who does not know where the stock of matches, the sack of potatoes, or even his own socks are kept in his house is very typical.

Help cannot be expected from the husband, not even in the way of setting the table or clearing away the dishes. You may think this is slavery. Turkish women think of it as sole ownership. With memories of the communal use of the house and husband of the Ottomans so fresh in the collective consciousness, the woman has to prove to society that she can possess and cope alone. Also, the culture still nourishes the idea that a man who helps his wife in the house is not a 'manly man' so even those who do share some of the work stop doing it when they have company. On the other hand, I have heard many women interpreting this situation as evidence of their superiority: "He messes everything up and I have to do the job again after him," they say, "so I might as well do it myself."

THE ELDERLY

Couples who start their home have the house all to themselves and their children until help is needed by their parents as they become old, frail and lonely. Some institutional care exists but putting the elderly away is not looked upon positively by society. Instead they are taken care of by their families. There are no community pastime schemes organised for the old people, who are left to their own resources to fill in the time. Mostly they become stationary in the house, providing some help with light housework but more importantly love and moral support for the younger family members.

BIRTH

During pregnancy, photographs of beautiful girls and handsome boys are placed in the expectant mother's room as it is believed that the new baby will be as good looking if the mother sees only perfect images. Another belief is that the new baby is susceptible to evil forces within the first 40 days after birth, when it is best for the mother and her baby to stay indoors and accept visitors. One of the common presents to bring on such occasions is a gold coin, the size and thickness of which depends on the buyer's pocket and relationship with the family. Clothes and toys for the baby are common too. Proud parents advertise the birth in newspapers, usually thanking the doctor or the midwife who helped with the delivery.

The saying: "A manly man has a manly son," sums up the father's expectations. Indeed, as carriers of the family name and fortune, the sons are more valued than daughters, but this tendency sometimes brings unexpected results. I heard in Marmaris, a place which used to be inconspicuous even for the Turks 15 years ago but which since then has become one of the most internationally popular and rich resort towns on the Aegean coast, that most elderly locals were tearing out their hair in despair. Apparently in the past they had left their inland fields to their sons for cultivation, and their seaside lands, which were not suitable for growing crops and therefore considered useless, to their daughters. Now the sons are still sowing potatoes and onions while the daughters and sons-in-law are rolling in money because of the luxury hotels built on their property.

DEATH

Just like birth, death is announced in the papers, but while birth advertisements are not too eye catching, those advertising deaths can be very prominent indeed, depending on the wealth of the family. Sometimes different advertisements for the same person, put in by his immediate family, close relatives, friends and even his colleagues can take up a whole page, leaving room for nothing else.

The dead must be buried without much delay, especially in the summer, so only a day or two is allowed for the relatives in distant locations to make their way to the funeral. The corpse is washed, perfumed and shrouded by professionals before it is taken to a mosque where the ceremony is held. The Imam (a religious leader) reads from the Koran and asks those who are gathered there, "How did you know this person?" They all say, "We knew him to be a good man or woman." This is to give a clean start to the person on his or her last journey. After the ceremony the bereaved family hold a funeral dinner for the relatives, friends, the religious officials involved in the funeral and some poor people.

Those attending a funeral wear dark, formal clothes and women have their heads covered. No presents are taken there and the custom of sending wreaths has gradually changed to making donations to charities or planting a tree in the name of the deceased.

Graveyards

Graveyards are distinguished by the white marble tombstones which bear the name as well as the dates of birth and death of the deceased. In the Ottoman times, different officials had different headgear and it was customary to have the same headgear carved on top of the tombstone to indicate the dead person's professional background. This is not practised any longer but the passengers in a boat travelling down the Bosporus can see today rows and rows of these turbaned tombstones in the old graveyards scattered along the sea banks, as if the Ottomans have risen from their death beds to watch solemnly over what has become of their beloved city.

CHILDREN

When you arrive in Turkey you will notice that the children are not only seen but heard there. They will be everywhere – in the streets, gardens, construction sites, shopping areas, balconies, entrance halls of the blocks of apartments, on the garden walls. This does not change with the season either. Even in winter, when you think they will be at school you are mistaken. Many schools operate on a shift system with independent morning and afternoon sessions, so while half of the school population is tucked away in the classrooms, the other half is out, either having completed the work for the day or waiting for their turn to come. But I prefer to see the children of Turkey as privileged and underprivileged rather than belonging to morning and afternoon groups.

The privileged are born to well-to-do families and doting parents. Those in this group are waited upon and in some cases chased by their frustrated mothers, who follow them with a plate in their hand and a plea, "Come on, have one more," while the spaghetti is dangling from the fork or the yoghurt is dripping from the spoon, as if the fugitives would die of hunger if they did not eat this last mouthful.

The underprivileged on the other hand live in crowded households and have to go out to work during off-school hours to help their parents, who are otherwise unable to make ends meet. These children will polish your shoes, wipe clean the windows of your car, carry your shopping for you from the market place, sell you a lottery ticket or a newspaper, and in the end, they often turn out to be more successful adults than those who have spent their childhood dodging their mothers' spoons.

Circumcision

Circumcision is the only religious ritual that all Turkish boys undergo. Other religious practices such as going on a pilgrimage, attending the mosque on Fridays, fasting during Ramadan and being kosher can be waived but an uncircumcised Turkish man is unheard of.

Boys between the ages of 5 and 15 have this operation, which is considered to be a turning point from childhood into manhood, similar to the Jewish Barmitzvah. It is usually done sometime in spring or late summer when the weather is comfortably warm and can include several boys from the same family, or boys from poor families who cannot afford to hold a party on their own. Although some people have it done at home, it is more customary for a hall to be hired and relatives to be invited for a meal.

Starting from days before the operation and until the circumcision day, the boys wear white trousers and a white shirt, adorned with a bright red sash carrying the word *Masallah* (May God preserve him from evil) and complete with a white cap. Partly proud of their importance for the period and partly in awe of what is to come, these little boys stroll about in the streets with their parents and show off their special clothes to other envious boys whose turn is yet to come. They can do all the mischief their hearts desire too, in the knowledge that this is probably the only time in their lives that they will go unpunished.

After the operation there is entertainment for the circumcised children while the guests give their presents to the boys. The presents from the parents are in accordance with the importance of the event, a gold watch, a bicycle, a computer, an electric train set or something of similar value. The guests, however, are not expected to go to such lengths but if you are invited, bring toys or items of a modest value.

PROFESSIONS

Popular professions in Turkey depend on what is fashionable at the time. In the Ottoman days, low-salaried but secure jobs were in demand. Dealing with money or the fine arts was considered to be abject, so all educated Turks dreamed of either the army or civil service work, leaving the trading and the artistic achievements to the Armenians, the Greeks and the Jews.

After the republic, Atatürk declared that the peasants were the masters of the country. Encouraged by this, most Anatolians who used to work for a landlord got hold of a patch of ground and turned to farming. This did not last long. Industrial changes in the western cities, especially in and around Istanbul, attracted people to universities to study for professional jobs like engineering, business and medicine. While cities were thus being inflated with the constant migration from the countryside, the job of building contractor *(müteahhit)* became an attractive one. Then came the computer age and now there seem to be almost as many computer programmers in Turkey as there are computers.

The Turks like professional titles and the more impressive they are the better. In the 1960s it was trendy to be an architect *(mimar)* but after a while this did not seem to be enough when all of a sudden architect-engineers *(mimar-mühendis)* came on the scene. This was followed by the senior architect-engineers *(yüksek mimar-mühendis)*, the seniority being gained as a result of longer years of education at university level.

Another impressive word is *müdür* (manager) and the abundance of them in all sectors makes me wonder where the people under these managers are. One example is that everybody employed in a sales department seems to be a sales manager *(satış müdürü)*, whereas I have yet to meet a salesman *(satış elemanı)*.

I remember an unemployed friend of mine giving me a visiting card for his telephone number. Underneath his name, his position was given as "Director." I could not suppress the temptation to challenge him on this point. "Come on now," I said, "directorship is not a profession, it is only a position, and without a company to direct, the position does not exist. How can you be a director?" He was not impressed by my logic. "If I were to work somewhere, my experience and age would not let me accept anything below this position," he said, "so I'm a director, with or without a company." I was not impressed by his logic either.

EDUCATION

Primary education starts at the age of seven and lasts for five years. The next stage is the so-called middle school, paving the way to the high school, or *lycée*, as in France, which is where the Turkish educational system comes from. Both are of three years duration.

State schools lack on financial aid and have many drawbacks as a result. The private schools claim to offer better facilities and

Turkish schoolchildren hard at work honing their reading skills. (Photo: Turkish Tourist Office)

43

educational standards but are limited in number and expensive for most people. Despite this, there is a big demand for them, so they regulate student intake with an entrance examination. Students take yet another examination later on for a place at university. As entry to both good schools and universities is thus limited, the children go to private institutions or tutors after the official school hours, to prepare themselves for the hurdles which lie ahead.

SUPERSTITIONS

There are many superstitions in Turkey and even educated people are not completely immune to them.

Although it is illegal to make a commercial practice of, for example, casting a spell, doing magic, breathing on sick people in order to cure them or telling fortunes, a large portion of the society believes in and turns to such practices in desperation.

Evil Eye

The most widespread belief is to do with the evil eye *(nazar)*. As human beings, we are all supposed to feel envious upon seeing or hearing something nice, something which others have and we do not. It is believed that this feeling of envy may cause harm to the things envied. People with green or blue eyes are said to be especially dangerous. As a result, other people's property and good news are not praised without the protective word *Masallah* (May God preserve) and children as well as property are equipped with a blue bead in the shape of an eye to ward off the effects of the evil eye.

If you see a woman (it is a characteristically feminine gesture) pulling the lobe of her ear and squeezing her lips to give out a pressurised kissing sound at the same time, you can be sure that she has just recounted some fortunate story. With this combined act of movement and sound, she is sending a 'bullet to the devil's ears' in the hope that it will be the bullet that reaches them rather than her good words.

Another custom is to pour water from a jug as people are leaving to wish them a safe journey. Shoes are not left with one sitting on top of the other as it is inviting trouble to tangle the feet of the owner. Before starting anything risky or dangerous, one says *"Bismillah"* (In the name of God) and takes the first step with the right leg.

Sharp items such as a knife or a pair of scissors are deadly and believed to carry harmful *djinns*. They should not be handed straight over to someone else but left on a surface, from where the other person takes them. If putting them down is not possible at least give them a gentle spit to scare off the *djinns*, before handing them over.

You are supposed to smile as soon as you see the new moon in the sky and the month will bring you pleasant things to keep you smiling until the next crescent moon appears.

There are superstitions concerning animals too. It is believed that killing a spider will bring bad luck, as will seeing a black cat or an owl. The last two have correlations with the night, one because of its colour, the other because of its nocturnal nature, and indeed the night is feared with all its uncertainties and secrets. Housewives never do housework after the sun is set in case there are dark souls lurking in the shadowy corners.

There are also superstitions which are international such as avoiding passing underneath a ladder and the number 13, which is hard to find on a house in the street. Another number people avoid using on their houses is 100 and you will note that after 98 comes 102. This, however, is for fear of public ridicule rather than of the supernatural – *yüz numara* (the number one hundred) is a euphemism for a toilet.

— *Chapter Three* —

COMMUNICATION

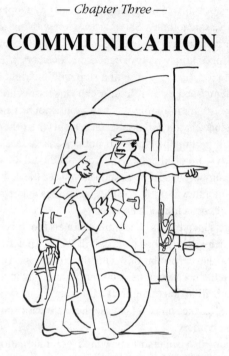

A different world awaits you in Turkey. Not only will the visual things around you be unusual in colour, shape and texture, the sounds will not be what you are used to either. Perhaps for the first time in your life you will hear the cries of street vendors, the call to prayer from the loudspeakers on the minaret, crickets chirruping in the silence of the night, the whistles of the night-watchmen, here and there a mixture of oriental songs and disco music pouring out into the air. You cannot divorce what you see around you from what you hear. In order to appreciate this country, you need to make sense of all these and a lot more. And of course, primarily, you need to become familiar with some, at least, of the most meaningful combination of sounds – the language.

SPEAKERS OF TURKISH

Turkish is a member of the Turkic language family, spoken by roughly 125 million people all around the world. Nearly 60 million of these are in mainland Turkey. There are said to be as many living in the Central Asian republics. In addition, there are almost three million Turkish workers living in Germany, Belgium and the Netherlands collectively, some in Northern Cyprus, and some 250,000 in England, as well as smaller groups in countries like Bulgaria, Greece, Macedonia, Albania, Romania, Syria, Iraq and Iran. The wide spread of Turkic speaking people is not surprising when one remembers two important historical facts: the Turks originally migrated from Central Asia to the west, and some of them settled down on the way, before the rest reached Anatolia. This explains the existence of Turkic language speaking people in today's Kazakistan, Kirgizistan, Azerbeijan, Tajikistan, Turkmenistan and Uzbekistan.

Another fact to bear in mind is that the Ottoman Empire, out of which the present Turkish Republic has emerged, was the largest empire in the world in the 16th century, with its boundaries stretching from Central Asia in the east to the neighbourhoods of Vienna in the west, and extending in the south to what is known today as Syria, Iraq, Egypt, Morocco, Algeria, Yemen, Oman, and Saudi Arabia. The empire of the old days was like a huge ocean which, in time, contracted into a smaller sea – the present Turkey – leaving, just like an ocean, lakes and ponds here and there, all over Eastern Europe and the Middle East.

HOW TO COMMUNICATE WITH THE TURKS

Speakers of English should not be worried about communication problems, as in almost all big cities, they will find people who are enthusiasts for English. French and German are also spoken, although they are not as popular as English. Italian and Spanish speakers are not easy to come by, even in the large cities.

If you are an English language speaker, you may be approached at your table or in the middle of the street by passers-by who are eager to practise with you what little they know of your language.

It has to be said, however, that should you utter something in Turkish to the Turks they will be delighted. Even a simple *"merhaba,"* (hello) will do the trick. They will relax and smile immediately and look at you in wonder as if you have done something extremely difficult.

LEARNING TURKISH

If you are going to live in the country for a long time, you will be advised to learn the language through formal teaching. You can either find someone to help you with this in exchange for lessons in your own language, or better still, you can go to a language teaching institution.

Your embassy or consulate will no doubt be helpful in recommending a reliable establishment, depending on which city you are going to settle in. A reputable Turkish language teaching institution in Ankara is TOMER, with branches in several other cities, and you might also like to contact them for suggestions. On the other hand, you may prefer to learn the language before you go to Turkey, in which case you are advised to get yourself one of the self-teaching books and cassettes available on the market. Some of these are listed at the back of this book. In any case, you will find the following introduction to the language useful.

THE TURKISH LANGUAGE

Turkish is an agglutinative language, like Finnish and Hungarian. Agglutination means you have a base on to which you add other items and with each addition the meaning changes slightly. For example, *Bayrak* is "flag" and *Bayraktar* is "flag bearer." *Ogul* is "son" and when this item is attached to the same combination you get

Bayraktaroglu, "the son of a flag bearer." You may think this is no different from what happens in English or German under the linguistic description of inflexion: add "less" to "care" and you have "careless," add "ness" to this, and you end up with "carelessness." Similarly in German, *Freund-lich-keit* (friend-li-ness) is a word which consists of three parts. The difference with agglutination is that, using the same method, you can have complete sentences which are no more than a single word. For example, *gelmiyorlardı* can be broken into pieces as follows:

gel-m-iyor-lar-dı

gel	verb stem for "to come"
mi	particle for negation
iyor	particle for progressive tense
lar	particle for third person plural
dı	particle for past tense

When all these are put together, you have the sentence: "They were not coming," which is only one word in Turkish. Very economical, some may think.

The word order is different from that of most languages of Latin and Anglo-Saxon origin. For example, the English sentence: I (subject) wrote (verb) a letter (object), can be translated into Turkish as: *Ben* (subject) *mektup* (object) *yazdım* (verb).

As these examples show, the word order in English is S+V+O whereas it is S+O+V in Turkish. For this reason, it is said that doing simultaneous translation from Turkish into English is more difficult than translating from, say, French, which has a word order similar to that of English. This is because in Turkish, one has to wait for the main verb to arrive, and as this is at the end of the sentence, one cannot start translating before the sentence is complete.

The Turks adopted the Latin alphabet in 1928 but had to make some changes to fit it into their sound system. The result was as follows:

Aa	*as in*	f<u>u</u>n	**Bb**	*as in*	<u>b</u>us
Cc		<u>J</u>im	**çç**		<u>ch</u>ild
Dd		<u>d</u>oor	**Ee**		f<u>e</u>stive
Ff		<u>f</u>ar	**Gg**		<u>g</u>o
ğğ		(This is soft g which only indicates that the preceding vowel is a lengthened one.)			
Hh		<u>h</u>at	**ıı**		comm<u>o</u>n
Ii		t<u>i</u>n	**Jj**		plea<u>s</u>ure
Kk		<u>c</u>omb	**Ll**		<u>l</u>ip
Mm		<u>m</u>other	**Nn**		<u>n</u>ot
Oo		<u>o</u>n	**öö**		<u>gi</u>rdle
Pp		<u>p</u>aper	**Rr**		<u>r</u>ope
Ss		<u>s</u>oap	**Şş**		<u>sh</u>ort
Tt		<u>t</u>able	**Uu**		f<u>u</u>ll
üü		*Fr.* D<u>u</u>pont	**Vv**		<u>v</u>oltage
Yy		<u>y</u>oung	**Zz**		<u>z</u>ebra

You may already have noted that the letters W and X do not exist in this alphabet simply because Turkish does not have the W sound, and X is thought to be superfluous when one can use "ks" as in *faks* and *taksi*.

Reading and Writing Turkish

The language is easy to read as each letter represents a sound and the logic is that if the letter is there the sound will be too and vice versa. Because of this correlation between the sounds and letters in their language, the Turks do not need to ask one another, for instance, how their names are spelt. The assumption is that they will be spelt as they are heard.

So far you may have got the impression that you will have no difficulty in writing down a word you hear, even if you do not know what it means. Not quite. Although the explanation given above represents the ideal situation, not every speaker will pronounce the words as they should be pronounced. It is quite possible to hear someone say *di mi* and even if you cleverly interpret this as a question tag like, "Isn't it …?" do not try to write it down as *di mi*. The correct written form is *degil mi*. What happened to the perfect correlation we were talking about? you may ask. The correlation still exists, although people may change the sounds, especially in connected speech, depending on where they come from, where they live, how familiar they are with you, how formal or informal the context is, and how educated they are.

USEFUL WORDS AND PHRASES

There is obviously no substitute for actually taking the plunge and studying the language. Nor will a phrase-book, no matter how substantial, fully integrate you into the verbal complexities of Turkish culture but the few following words and phrases will help you along in the initial stages.

Loan Words

There are many words in Turkish taken from other languages. The Turks like to give credit where credit is due and borrow the words from the nations which offer the most useful examples. For example, the Spanish are considered to talk a lot, so *palavra* (Spanish: *palabra*) is used to mean blarney or palaver. *Makarna* (spaghetti) is taken from the Italians, the best spaghetti makers. To give credit to the Germans as the best motorway system owners, they call their own motorways *otoban* (German: *autobahn*).

In the 19th century the French came to Anatolia, commissioned to construct the country's railroads, the bulk of which are still in use today, including the famous Edirne-Baghdad route. Not only did the French do the railroads, they also brought with them the vocabulary necessary for this new form of travelling. *Tren* (train), *gar* (main train station building), *istasyon* (station), *gise* (ticket office), *bilet* (ticket), *peron* (platform), *kondüktör* (ticket collector) have thus entered into Turkish. The event set a trend and thereafter further French words for other forms of transport were also adopted, such as *otobüs* (bus), *kamyon* (truck), *bisiklet* (bicycle), *motosiklet* (motorcycle) and *traktör* (tractor).

In the 20th century, English words started overtaking the French, especially in the areas of business and technology. And, of course in the case of football, English words have the unquestionable dominance, as *gol* (goal), penaltı (penalty), *haftaym* (half-time), *ofsayd* (offside) and *lig* (league) evidently show.

On the other hand, some English words have undergone a change and the derivation is not so evident. Can you guess what *forvet* is? It is the forward striker in football. *Biftek?* It is beef steak. *Rozbif?* It is roast beef, of course.

Do not think, however, that all English words in Turkish, whether used in full or in a modified form, mean what they mean in English. If you ask for *çips* in a restaurant, you will be given crisps, and if you order *pasta* you will be brought a cream cake. *Gazino* is simply a tea-garden and *apartman* is a block of flats. As for *limonata,* you will get a very sweet and still drink made of lemon juice. If you really want lemonade, ask for *gazoz* but if this is all too complicated, just stick to a cold *bira* (beer) or *koka kola*.

For Socialising

You will most likely encounter all, or at least some, of the following conversational elements in the early stages of your stay in Turkey. Nothing will assist your settling in more than showing the locals that you are making an effort to master some of the local language.

First Speaker	**Second Speaker**
Merhaba	*Merhaba*
Hello	Hello
Günaydın	*Günaydın*

Good morning
Iyi aksamlar
Good evening
Iyi geceler
Good night
Tesekkür ederim
Thank you
Nasılsınız?
How are you?

Good morning
Iyi aksamlar
Good evening
Iyi geceler
Good night
Estagfurullah, bir sey, degil*
Don't mention it, it's nothing
Iyiyim, tesekkür ederim.
I'm well, thank you
Siz nasılsınız?
And you?

Ben de iyiyim, tesekkür ederim
I'm well too, thank you
Hos geldiniz
Welcome
(said by the host/ess)
Allahaısmarladık
Good bye
Affedersiniz
I'm sorry
Serefinize
To your honour
(in drinking a toast)

Hos bulduk
Well we have found
(set response to Hos geldiniz)
Güle güle
Go happily
Estagfurullah *
That's all right/Don't mention it
Serefinize
And to yours

* For a better understanding of these responses, see the explanation of *Estagfurullah* on pages 62–63.

Numbers

One/*Bir*	Two/*IKi*	Three/*Üç*
Four/*Dört*	Five/*Bes*	Six/*Altı*
Seven/*Yedi*	Eight/*Sekiz*	Nine/*Dokuz*

Ten/*On*	Eleven/*Onbir*	Twelve/*Oniki*
Twenty/*Yirmi*	Thirty/*Otuz*	Forty/*Kırk*
Fifty/*Elli*	Sixty/*Altmıs*	Seventy/*Yetmis*
Eighty/*Seksen*	Ninety/*Doksan*	
100/*Yüz*	101/*Yüzbir*	102/*Yüziki*
200/*Ikiyüz*	300/*Üçyüz*	
1,000/*Bin*	2,000/*Ikibin*	3,000/*Üçbin*
1,000,000/*Milyon*	2,000,000/*Iki milyon*	

Now you can read any number in Turkish by combining the ones given above. For example:

88 (80 + 8) – *Seksen sekiz*

135 (100 + 30 + 5) – *Yüz otuz bes*

3549 – *Üç bin bes yüz kırk dokuz*

132,631 – *Yüz otuz iki bin, altı yüz otuz bir*

5,840,258 – *Bes milyon, sekiz yüz kırk bin, iki yüz elli sekiz*

Day and Time References

Monday/*Pazartesi*	Tuesday/*Salı*	Wednesday/*Çarsamba*
Thursday/*Persembe*	Friday/*Cuma*	Saturday/*Cumartesi*
Sunday/*Pazar*		
Today/*Bugün*	Tomorrow/*Yarın*	Yesterday/*Dün*
Now/*Simdi*	Later/*Sonra*	This week/*Bu hafta*

Months

January/*Ocak*	February/*Subat*	March/*Mart*
April/*Nisan*	May/*Mayıs*	June/*Haziran*
July/*Temmuz*	August/*Agustos*	September/*Eylül*
October/*Ekim*	November/*Kasım*	December/*Aralık*

The date when written is set out in the following way: 3 Ocak Persembe (3 January Thursday).

Evet and Hayır

Most modern languages have only monosyllabic words for "Yes" and "No," such as the German *Ja/Nein*; the Italian and Spanish *Si/No*; the French *Oui/Non*; the Russian *Da/Niet;* and the Japanese *Hai/Iie* . For some reason, which is impossible to explain, in the Turkish language these words are accorded two syllables – *E-vet* for "Yes" and *Ha-yır* for "No."

If you think they will be difficult to remember, at least for "No," you might prefer using the alternative, *Yok*, which is more common in informal speech.

FORMS OF ADDRESS

Names

Only very close people call one another by their first names, and only if they are more or less of the same age. In the case of an age gap, seniority is marked by an additional polite address form such as *Hanım* for a female – as in *Ayse Hanım*, or *Bey* for a male – as in *Ahmet Bey*. This also applies to people who are not socially close. Professional titles may take the lead in the sequence, as in *Doktor Ali Bey*.

During the modernisation period, new address forms have come into use: *Bay* (masculine) and *Bayan* (feminine) which precede the names – *Bay Ahmet Kaya* and *Bayan Ayse Kaya*. This is used to write names on an envelope. To make it more polite, another word, *Sayın* (Esteemed) can be added to the rest – *Sayın Bay Ahmet Kaya* or *Sayın Bayan Ayse Kaya*. This is definitely used when one is addressing or referring to people who hold high governmental offices. You may also find the words *Bay* and *Bayan* on the public conveniences.

Social or affectionate closeness between people is communicated through the use of family relation terms. For example, if one person calls another *Ahmet Amca* (Uncle Ahmet) or *Ayse Teyze* (Aunt Ayse), it does not necessarily mean that they are related. The same ploy is used to indicate that there is no sexual motive in a conversational

gambit, that one's intentions are purely innocent and family-like. It is quite acceptable for a salesman to call a passing woman to his shop by saying, *"Abla, gel su mallara bir bak"* (Big sister, come and have a look at these goods) or *"Teyze, karpuz istiyor musun?"* (Aunty, would you like to have some watermelons?)

Sen and Siz

As there are *tu* and *vous* in French, and *du* and *sie* in German, in Turkish too, there are two pronouns for the word "you," with different levels of formality: *sen* for the second person singular, and *siz* for the second person plural.

A clear-cut definition would state that sen is used when one is addressing a single person, and *siz* for two or more. However, in practice it is not as simple as this, because *siz* can also be used to a single addressee as long as certain conditions are satisfied, namely age, social distance and social status. In other words, if the person you are talking to is older or higher in status than you are, *siz* is definitely a must. Similarly, you can use *siz* if you feel that you are not yet socially close to the person you are conversing with.

In the cases of age and social status, there is an asymmetric distribution of pronouns between the speakers. What this means is that, while you should address the person who is older than you are, or who holds a higher social status than you do, as *siz*, he or she will address you as *sen*. This asymmetry does not obtain when social distance is involved. If you and your interlocutor are not on familiar terms, you should both use *siz*. Now this may lead to some difficult decisions in choosing the right pronoun. How do you address the taxi driver, for instance. You may choose to call him *sen* if you feel that his social status is lower than yours, but *siz* may be appropriate if you have not met him before. It is a personal choice that you have to make here.

Social distance creates another fuzzy area. Those who are newly acquainted should use *siz* to one another but two people cannot stay newly acquainted forever. As time goes by familiarity increases and this justifies a switch to *sen*. But now we have the problem of timing the change-over. When is the right point in time to call an acquaintance a 'friend' and promote him or her to *sen*? If you are in quandary over this, the safest bet is to leave the decision to the Turkish native speaker. It is better to stay on formal terms than make a social gaffe.

The formal use of *siz* to a single addressee is an urban practice. You will notice in the rural areas that *sen* and *siz* have only one function, and this is the one explained in the clear-cut definition above. If you address someone in the rural area as *siz* out of respect, politeness or on the assumption that you do not know him at all, he will not understand why you are referring to him as such and will look around to see who else is there, apart from himself, to justify this plurality.

USEFUL LINGUISTIC FUNCTIONS

The following phrases will help you in the early stages of your stay in Turkey to get around and ask simple directions (and understand the replies). From here you can build on your knowledge and before long, with a little perseverence, you will be able to have complete conversations in Turkish.

Requests

The following phrases will help you in hotels, airports and restaurants:

* *istiyorum, lütfen*
I would like (to have) *, please

* *bir sise su*	a bottle of water
* *bir kutu aspirin*	a box of aspirins
* *iki kisilik bir oda*	a double room
* *Ankara ya gidis-dönüs bir bilet*	a return ticket to Ankara
* *hesabı*	the bill
* *dolar degistirmek*	to exchange dollars
* *bu adrese gitmek*	to go to this address
* *burada inmek*	to get off here

Offers and Thanks

Alır mısınız?
Would you like to take (this)?
Buyrun, lütfen
Please, have (one, some)

And importantly:
Tesekkür ederim
Thank you
Hayır, tesekkür ederim
No, thank you

Reporting Faults

* *bir problem var*
There is a problem (fault) *

* *telefonda*	in the telephone
* *anahtarda*	in the key/in the lock
* *sıcak suda*	in the hot water (system)
* *dusta*	in the shower
* *televizyonda*	in the television
* *muslukta*	in the tap

Asking for Directions

*En yakın * nerede acaba*
Where is the nearest *, I wonder

* *otel*	hotel
* *banka*	bank
* *otobüs duragı*	bus stop
* *taksi duragı*	taxi stop
* *postahane*	post office
* *hastahane*	hospital
* *süpermarket*	supermarket
* *turist danısma*	tourist information

Of course, there is no point in asking your way if you don't know the words which you will hear from the helper who directs you. Some of the possibilities are:

sagda	on the right
solda	on the left
asagıda	down there
yukarıda	up there
orada	there
biraz ileride	a bit further down
karsıda	opposite
kösede	at the corner

Requesting a Closer Look at Something

suna bakabilir miyim, lütfen?
May I have a look at that, please?
Bunu gösterir misiniz, lütfen?
Will you show me this, please?
Bunu deneyebilir miyim?
May I try this on?

Asking the Price of Something

Bu kaça?
How much is this?
Onun fiyatı ne?
What is the price of that?

Bargaining

Biraz indirim yapın lütfen
Please make some reduction in the price
Çok pahalı, alamam
It is very expensive, I can't afford it
* *Lira olsun*
Let it be for * Liras.
* (Say whatever you think is the reasonable price here.)

FORMULAIC EXPRESSIONS

There are many obligatory situational formulas in Turkish. These are used by everyone in the appropriate situation, and the failure to use them is regarded as a faux pas. Of course, this goes only for the Turks themselves, your ignorance of the formulas will be excused on the grounds that you are a visitor. But think how overjoyed they will be if you say the right words to the right people at the right time. The following list is at your disposal if you wish to make an exceptionally good impression in your new environment:

Gözünüz aydın	Your eye sparkling. (On receipt of good news.)
Basınız sagolsun	May your head be alive. (When someone dies.)
Güle güle giyin	Wear it laughingly. (When someone acquires a new article of clothing.)
Güle güle oturun	Stay laughingly. (When someone moves into a new house.)
Kolay gelsin	May it come easy. (When someone is busy with something.)
Elinize saglık	Health to your hands. (In appreciation of something prepared manually – most commonly used for food.)
Geçmis olsun	May it pass. (To a person who is sick or has recently recovered from illness.)
Sıhhatler olsun	May it be healthy. (After someone takes a bath or has had a haircut.)
Afiyet olsun	May it be healthy. (To start or finish a meal.)
Allah mesut etsin	May God make happy. (To a newlywed couple.)
Çok yasa	Live long. (To someone who has sneezed.)
Allah kavustursun	May God reunite. (On the departure of someone close.)
Zahmet olacak	It will be a trouble. (In asking for a favour.)
Kesenize bereket	Plenty to your purse. (To thank the host/ess after a meal.)
Bayramınız kutlu olsun	May your feast be merry. (At a religious or national feast day.)
Tebrik ederim	I congratulate.

ATTITUDES EXHIBITED THROUGH LANGUAGE

Masallah

You were introduced in the previous chapter to the widely popular artifact, the Blue Bead, which is believed to ward off the effects of evil eye. *Masallah,* meaning "praise god," is the linguistic equivalent of the same concept. In fact, a second name for the Blue Bead is *Masallah*.

It is a common belief that good news may create envy and should be protected from it. The word *Masallah* is the protective shield. If you wish to keep your Turkish friends happy, say *Masallah* after any piece of personal good news that you hear: A baby is born, *Masallah*; the son has passed his exams, *Masallah*; a husband has come back to his wife – Oooh, 41 times *Masallah*! Why 41 times? In Islam 40 is a lucky number, together with the numbers one, three and nine. Among the Turks of pre-Islamic days, it was also the unreachable number, like the 'umpteenth' in English. No matter which tradition has the stronger hold in this case, it is obvious that 41 makes *Masallah* impregnable.

Insallah

This roughly translates as "God willing." You may hope, or wish, or even be determined to do something, but what good is it if it is not according to the will of God? Although it was originally linked with the Islamic concept of fate, *Insallah* has in time acquired some non-religious functions.

An English father may say, "We'll see," to his child rather than make a strong commitment – "Shall we play football tomorrow, Daddy?" To which the father may reply, "Well, we'll see." The same applies to *Insallah*. You may not want to do something but you may not want to say this openly either. In such cases, say *Insallah* if you want to appear agreeable but at the same time leave the door open for inaction by passing the responsibility to the will of God. Who knows what God has willed, anyway?

Allahaskina

There is good news and bad news about the making of offers by Turkish people. The bad news is that they can be very stubborn in making them. This stubbornness is, however, exhibited on the understanding that the recipient of an offer should not immediately accept it. This often creates a conflict whereby one party insists on making an offer and the other refuses to accept it. Consequently, the person who makes the offer may become involved in a period of persuasion, lasting until one party gives in.

This persuasion can go through three stages, depending on how determined each party is to fulfil his social obligations. The first stage is when a reference is made to God with *Allahaskina* (For the love of God) as in, "Accept it for the love of God." If this does not work, a similar ploy can be tried – *Beni seviyorsan* (If you love me). If the recipient of the offer remains implacable, pressure is increased by a threat – *Konusmam* (I won't talk to you again), *Küserim* or *Darilirim* (I will cut all my ties with you). If these also prove unsuccessful, then the climax is reached with *Ölümü gör* (Over my dead body). No one should resist the offer once this has been said. Accept it even if it is anathema to you.

The good news is that not all offers go through these three stages. There will also be occasions when Turkish people feel that they should make an offer, knowing that it will be refused anyway and hoping that they will not be obliged to go through all the stages of persuasion. False assumptions, however, can sometimes bring unexpected results. I remember a friend complaining about a foreign visitor who admired her lighter and accepted it when it was offered to him. "I offered it half-heartedly (Turks say half-mouthedly for this – *yarim agiz*) and he accepted it without a second thought," she said.

Estagfurullah

The Ottoman palace system was a system of ranks which had its reflections in the language of the elite. Politeness in those days meant a continuous claim to inferiority for oneself and superiority for the other person. Either belittle yourself or give credit to whomever you are speaking to, and thus create an imbalance in the conversational equilibrium: such was the understanding behind it. This exaggerated style has eroded with time but has not disappeared altogether. Even today, one can find some remnants of this mentality in the language:

Emrinize amadeyim:	I am ready to receive your commands. (In offering one's help.)
Fakirhanemize seref verdiniz:	You have bestowed honour upon our poverty-stricken house. (In welcoming a guest.)
Ben elinize su bile dökemem:	I won't be suitable even to pour out water for you to wash your hands. (Claiming a mismatch between oneself and the other person.)
Basimin üstünde yeriniz var:	You have a place on top of my head. (Offering hospitality, meaning, "You can even sit on my head, if you want to.")
Acizane fikrimi sorarsaniz:	If you ask for my worthless opinion. (In making a point.)

So long as you are high in rank and therefore deserve to be exalted anyway, you can gracefully watch the other person make himself a doormat – or as in the example above, a divan cushion – for you. On the other hand, you may be on equal terms with your interlocutor, in which case you should do something to restore the balance that has now been momentarily destroyed. One way to rectify the situation is to offer a similar claim to inferiority, but note that the seesaw will then be tipped to your side and your partner will not allow you to sit comfortably with your feet on the ground while his are dangling up in the air. So, the motion will continue for goodness knows how many times. The second and more effective but at the same time polite way to stop this process is through *Estagfurullah*.

Estagfurullah is a loan word from Arabic, meaning, "I beg the pardon of God." You may wonder why God's pardon is needed at this point. The idea is that God is the only sublime being and we, as his inferior creatures, are all the same. Therefore, when a speaker creates imbalance in the conversation in the way explained above, the other person reminds him of his unchangeable place in this world, while at the same time appealing for God's forgiveness for the sin that has been committed.

No doubt, *Estagfurullah* came into Turkish on the wings of Islam but, like *Insallah*, over the centuries it has lost its religious connotations, and today it is used in a variety of situations, even after the most common, everyday balance-disturbing speech acts, such as thanks and apologies.

COMMUNICATION TOPICS

What to Talk About

The Turks do not normally talk about the weather. In any case, the weather, being almost always cold in the winter and hot in the summer, is so stable that it does not qualify as an interesting conversational topic. Instead, they favour the economic situation, politics, football and their children.

Make sure you know the recent inflation rate in your own country before you set off for Turkey because most probably you will be asked this for comparison. Inflation in Turkey has been on an upward curve since the 1950s, providing fodder for the political opposition, no matter who is in power. Today, every Turk is concerned with the rise in inflation and will know the current rate.

Money matters for the man in the street are not only confined to macro-economics. Don't be taken aback if you are asked how much you earn. Turks like boasting or complaining about their income, so here again, they like to have a basis for comparison.

Sensitive Subjects

There are some topics you should avoid and at the top of this list are Cyprus, Bosnia, the European Union and Human Rights. Although the Turks admire the West on very many fronts, they believe that there has been prejudice and injustice displayed by the Westerners when it comes to these subjects.

Although Turkey is a country where, as the tourism brochures will tell you, East meets West, there are still enough differences to make it advisable not to be too opinionated on certain subjects. This is obviously something you need to develop a feel for, so until you feel confident that the topic is not too touchy or likely to create offence, it is sometimes best to keep a low profile when certain issues, like the ones mentioned above, arise.

WHISTLE LANGUAGE

The fascinating phenomenon of the so-called whistle language in Turkey has attracted the attention of several linguists over the years but it must be said that this strange form of communication exists only in the Black Sea region, in a village called Kusköy (Bird's Village). People in this area communicate with each other through whistles, if the distance between them is beyond the reach of a shout. A visitor to the area once commented that she would like to know how a woman from Kusköy could make her husband come home from cutting wood in the forest, by simply whistling something to the effect that "Dinner is ready." She added, "I cannot get mine to come without calling him several times, even though I am using the more common form of communication and he is sitting in the next room."

BODY AND SIGN LANGUAGE

Except for those who are extremely religious and will not even shake hands with the opposite sex, Turks in general like touching or hugging one another in their social interaction. In conversation, they stand closer to each other than most Europeans do, too. It is worth knowing this, or you may find yourself progressing from one side of the room to another as you move backwards in a continuous attempt to re-establish what you feel is an appropriate distance between yourself and your Turkish partner.

Kissing

Social kissing on both cheeks is acceptable even between men. Do not jump to conclusions if you see one male kissing another on the cheek, because the social rules allow this.

There is also the kissing of the hand but this happens only when there is an age gap between the parties. The younger person firmly holds the hand of the older one, kisses the back of it and brings it up to his brow. The action is a sign of respect and carried out regardless

of the sex of either party. The kissing of a lady's fingers in the Western style is done but only in limited circles.

Sexual kissing in public is not approved of, as people think that this is something too private to be done in the open. Even at their wedding ceremony the groom kisses his bride either on the forehead or on the cheeks. Anything more intimate than this will be frowned upon as inconsiderate and impatient.

Meaningful Movements

Turkish people say "Yes" by a downward movement of the head. This can be done once or several times, with or without closing the eyes. The gesture for "No" is more confusing for the foreigner because, instead of shaking the head sideways, they move it backwards once, while at the same time raising their eyebrows. This action may be accompanied by clicking the tongue against the upper jaw. The shake of the head sideways means, "I don't know" but this is usually in conjunction with the raised shoulders and a protruded lower lip. A single jerk in one shoulder or both, on the other hand, communicates the message, "I don't care."

An expatriate, shortly after his arrival in Turkey, went into a shop in order to buy cigarettes. He asked for a pack but could not understand the muted response of the shop assistant who simply raised his eyebrows and tutted. When he got the same response after asking three times, he left the shop in bewilderment. It did not take him long to discover, however, that this was not something peculiar to this shop assistant – everybody tutted in Turkey to say "No."

There are several hand movements too. The shaking of the index finger up and down and pointed at you, while the rest of the fingers are closed, means, "I warn you," as it does in the English speaking societies. The hand moved to make circles in the air is to emphasise the countless occasions on which whatever is being talked about has been done. Joining the fingertips and kissing them collectively means "Wonderful." You will also notice that some people bring their right hand up to their chest in response to being asked, "How are you." This indicates that all is well with them.

There are also some other hand signs which we hope you will never have the chance to see, nor have to work out what they mean.

Chapter Four

SOCIAL LIFE IN TURKEY

SOCIALISING

As in many Mediterranean countries, where the summer is long and hot, in Turkey too, people spend most of their time in the open air – in their gardens or balconies, in the parks or streets or in the coffee houses, where socialisation is inevitable. In such places, old acquaintanceships can be renewed and new friendships formed very spontaneously – that is, as long as the approach does not come from a single man to a single woman. Otherwise, the Turks need no introduction to talk and once they start you will feel as if you have known them all your life. This out-of-doors sociability is continued throughout the winter in the form of house visits.

HOSPITALITY

Turkish people are renowned for their hospitality. Whatever their financial status, they welcome, and feed their guests as much as their resources allow. It may sound unbelievable but in Anatolia it is acceptable to knock on any door and ask for shelter, and it will be given, because unknown visitors are considered to be sent by God. This is, of course, too much to ask of the city dwellers who have lost trust in others after years of migration and the ensuing urban unrest. However, regardless of their geographical position, for all Turks hospitality is an almost religious task, which has to be accomplished in the best possible way and at any cost. Grace Ellison, who visited Turkey in the 1920s, when the relations between Turkey and England were quite strained, writes about an experience in her book, *An Englishwoman in Angora*. Half way through her visit to a Turkish home, her hostess apologises sadly and leaves with her little boy to go and see an ailing relative. The husband cooks, serves the meal and washes the dishes afterwards, being a perfect host all the way through. When it is time for Grace Ellison to leave, she sees tears in the eyes of her host and asks if she has offended him in some way. Only then does she learn that his brother-in-law died in the morning and his wife bravely set out alone to attend the funeral, while he stayed at home to attend the visitor. So, even the most intimate disaster was not permitted to interfere with hospitality and all this was done for an unknown woman from a hostile land.

Invitations

The Turks are very sensitive about leaving a positive impression, so it is not a good idea to visit them unexpectedly, unless you are a close friend who can use for this surprise appearance the excuse allowed only to very close friends: "I was passing by so I just called in." Instead, they like to know who is coming and when, well in advance, so that they can change into their best clothes, tidy the house and prepare the food. Unless it is a very formal occasion, like a circumci-

71

sion or a wedding party, they do not use invitation cards but prefer telephoning you or sending a third party, usually their children, to extend the invitation. They take pride in entertaining you at home rather than at a restaurant.

It is quite acceptable and normal for you to telephone them instead to ask if it is alright to visit them on a specific date. However, there is one point which needs some clarification, whether you are invited by them or you have invited yourself to their home – the Turks feel very uneasy about telling you when to arrive for the occasion. Even if you ask what time you should be there, they will find it extremely difficult to give you a direct answer and get around the question by a latitudinal answer like: "Any time after seven," or "Seven or eight, whenever." This is because specifying the time down to its minutes will sound as if you are unwelcome before or after this and such an implication is totally against their understanding of hospitality. In such cases, it is best to take the middle of the road and arrive at, say, 7:30.

It is not unusual for the Turks to extend impromptu invitations. If your visit somehow coincides with their meal time, they will probably ask you to stay and join in their 'modest' meal. Modest they will call it, but you can be sure that whatever is in their kitchen will be transferred to the table in your honour, no matter what original combinations this may lead to. I heard a visitor saying that in a village house she had been offered pieces of Turkish delight sandwiched between home-made biscuits. She asked me if this was common. It is not and I told her that but no doubt her ingenious hostess slept peacefully that evening, feeling that she had entertained her guest as well as her resources allowed.

House Visits

The streets in Turkey are dusty in the summer and muddy in the winter, so guests are supposed to take their shoes off on entering a traditional house. The hostess will object to this initially so as to give the guests a chance of saving face, in case they remember at the last minute that they forgot to change into a presentable pair of socks that morning. But if the guest properly insists on leaving the shoes by the threshold, slippers kept only for special occasions will be provided immediately.

The guests will then be ushered into the guest room. This is a sitting room which is closed to the family members at all times, except when they are entertaining. It contains the best furniture in the house as well as silver and crystal bric-a-brac to dazzle the visitors. The eldest or the most important visitor will be asked to sit in the 'prime corner' *(bas köse)* which does not need to be in a corner but will be the most prominent seat in the room and the farthest from the door. The Turks think that the distance from the door is significant in the sense that if you place your guest closer to the door, it will mean you wish him or her to be out as soon as possible. The nearest seat to the door is usually taken by the hostess herself.

In some traditional households it is still customary to open the conversation with ritualised welfare inquiries. What this means is that the eldest of the family will exchange with the eldest of the visiting party a sequence of "how-are-you"s and continue this with all the visitors in order of age or social importance, finally ending up with the children. Then the second eldest family member will take his or her turn. This will go on until every member of the household has exchanged welfare inquiries with everybody else in the room, although at the end everyone will have declared their state of health absurdly often.

Then will start the procession of offers, one after the other, with perhaps only ten minutes between them. In traditional households a round of eau-de-toilette will top the list. When the hostess or her daughter comes to you with a bottle of lemon or lavender scented eau-de-toilette just cup your hands to receive a generous splash. You are supposed to wet your wrists, neck, face and your hair with this. After being refreshed in this way, things to eat or drink will follow and the variety will depend on the season as well as the resources of the family. Tea, coffee, fruit juice, Turkish delight, chocolates, sweets, cakes, gateaux, sandwiches, pies, fruit, and ice-cream are some of the possibilities.

When should you take your leave? If you wait for an indication from your host, you will wait forever. The rules of hospitality will prevent him from giving any such sign. Even when he thinks it is high time you went, he will say, "What is the hurry? We have been siting and talking nicely." It is therefore up to you to decide on this matter but afternoon guests generally leave by 6.30 p.m. and evening guests no later than midnight.

While seeing you off, your host will hold your coat for you. This is a gesture of respect and should not be accepted readily. However, if the host insists to help you on with your coat, so be it. Just slip it on, thank your host and leave gracefully, with a feeling of content that in this household you are held in high esteem.

Giving and Receiving Presents

Not only on special occasions such as birthdays, anniversaries, weddings and circumcisions but even at a simple dinner party, people give and receive presents. This is no different from other cultures. What is specific to Turkey is the way presents change hands. Here, one needs some background information to understand the ritual.

By giving a present you are honouring the other person, so it has to be something appropriate to his or her status in your affections. On the other hand, the more valuable your present is, the more indebted the recipient will be to you for the honour. In short, it is a 'Catch-22' situation. What is the escape route? To buy something of a modest nature but present it with great deference. Or better still, do not present it at all but quietly leave it on a side-table or a chair in the hallway, as if you were ridding yourself of your shopping bag, to be collected on your way out. By doing this you are not giving your host the chance to thank you for something which you think does not deserve thanks anyway. In return, your host will pretend he has not seen you leaving a parcel there and will not remind you of it on your leave.

Alternatively, you can be so bold as to deposit your present in the hands of your host, but if you choose this option, humble yourself with the words, *"Size layık degil ama ..."* (This is not worthy of you but ...). Nobody ever finishes this sentence but it is regarded as a compliment in that you would consider no gift could match the regard you have for that person.

If you have put your presentation on record like this, your host will mumble something to the effect that, "You have troubled yourself a lot," and possibly will leave the parcel on the side-table or the chair in the hallway which you might have chosen yourself in the first place. Unless it is clearly a box of chocolates which has to be opened and offered to the guests, or flowers which have to be put in water, unwrapping the gift in the presence of the giver is not customary. The giver has humbled himself enough, why rub salt into the wound with further thanks? This will also save the recipient from absurdities such as, "Golly, this is just what I have always wanted. Thank you a million times."

The bottle of wine, which a dinner guest usually comes with in some European countries, does not enjoy the same popularity in Turkey. Instead, chocolates, fruit or flowers are the conventional presents.

And finally a word of caution on buying flowers for a lady. There should always be an odd number of flowers in the bunch – seven roses, nine carnations, eleven gladioli or whatever. The reason? Nobody knows but I guess this is a delicate way of paying a compliment. Why, together with the lady, does the odd number not make an even one?

FOOD

The Turks are very creative people when it comes to food. Although the country is surrounded by seas on three sides, fish does not enjoy overriding popularity. Instead, vegetables, meat, rice and pastry are the main features of the Turkish cuisine. With vegetables especially, they work miracles. It is said that there are at least fifty ways to cook aubergines. It is a very time consuming way of cooking too, with all the chopping, wrapping and stuffing of individual items, but the amount of time taken does not seem to worry anybody. The easy-going, never-hurry philosophy which prevails in almost every aspect of life, rules over their gastronomical affairs too. The Turks say they live to cook and eat, rather than cook and eat to live.

VEGETABLES AND FRUIT

Vegetables and fruit are rich in kind and plentiful. Things come in such abundance that Turkish people are somewhat spoilt and they buy everything in kilos and sometimes even in crates. Ask for a single cucumber or a banana and the greengrocer will look at you in disbelief. Speaking of cucumbers, some visitors should be warned about the size of these. Cucumbers in Turkey are smaller but tastier than those found in most Mediterranean countries. So are the aubergines and green peppers. On the other hand, tomatoes, watermelons, parsley, and peaches are very large. The peaches, especially those from the Bursa region, must be tried. Just squeeze them gently from both sides and the halves will fall open into your hands. They are juicy, tasty and filling – a far cry from the European peaches, which in some cases would be better used as tennis balls.

Although fruit and vegetables are produced in large quantities and varieties in the hot season, people are deprived of all this in the long winter months, so fruit is preserved as marmalades and jams. Particularly noteworthy among these are the rose petal, fig and morello cherry jams. Vegetables are used to make pickles. Alternatively, they are put on a string and dried under the sun so that they can be stored away for the winter. While travelling along the steppes of Anatolia, it is very picturesque to see the otherwise dull village houses, with rows and rows of red peppers on the balconies, shining brightly in the sunlight.

Vegetables that are cooked in olive oil are eaten cold but if stewed with meat, they are served hot. With all its cold vegetables, salads, pickles and dips of yoghurt or other things, Turkey is a vegetarian's paradise.

Dolma

Stuffed vegetables, called *dolma*, are an important part of the Turkish cuisine. Nothing which can be wrapped up or filled with a stuffing is spared. Aubergines, courgettes, green and red peppers, tomatoes, vine and cabbage leaves and many others all fall into this category and are prepared by all Turkish cooks.

Preparing wrapped vegetables is a challenge for the inexperienced, new cook but in time and with practice one gets better and quicker at it. So much so that some people are praised for being able to wrap up stuffings in vegetable leaves with only one hand. Of course, such manual wizardry is not within everybody's capacity, nor have many people the patience any more to reach such giddy culinary heights.

In this age when women are expected to fulfil all sorts of commitments, from housework to professional duties, from motherhood to looking after the elderly, even the basic knowledge of how to cook *dolmas* is enough to turn a man's head, as Holly Chase recounts in her book, *Turkish Tapestry*. This was her experience on the first day of her visit to the country:

During the next twelve hours, I was carried through the city in old DeSoto taxis and befriended by Talyan, a middle-aged sports writer on a right-wing newspaper. First, I installed myself in a very basic hotel of his recommendation. Then he took me out to dinner at a fashionable Bosphorus restaurant and asked me to marry him after I had innocently volunteered that I knew how to make stuffed grape leaves.

A *Quick Selection*

The selection and variety of food in Turkey makes it something of a gourmet's delight. The following dishes are just a small sample of the available delicacies in Turkey, but are a good place to begin your culinary voyage through the country.

Börek – Made out of thin layers of pastry, *börek* is one of the things that a visitor should try. There are two ways of making it – either on a baking tray with several layers of pastry, separated from one another with mixtures of grated cheese, eggs and parsley or minced beef, chopped onions and parsley, then cooked in the oven; or by wrapping small pieces of pastry around a piece of filling and then frying each piece individually, as one does with Chinese spring rolls. The pastry used is a special one *(yufka)* and can be bought from the patisserie *(pastahane)* or the bakery *(fırın)*.

Döner Kebab – Marinated lamb (minced meat is also used) on a vertical spit is grilled as it slowly turns next to the fire. The cooked slices are then cut with a huge knife and arranged on pitta bread or a heap of rice and served with some garnish and tomatoes. The alternative way of serving the meat together with salad inside a pitta bread has enjoyed worldwide popularity and competes well with other kinds of fast food.

Köfte – Finely minced meat with almost no fat is mixed with grated onions, parsley, eggs and spices and shaped differently. Some are round and small, some are oblong and some are flat. They are either grilled or fried or cooked in a sauce.

Pilav – *Pilav* is the way rice, cracked wheat or vermicelli is cooked with water and a generous knob of butter. The end result is a meal of individual grains rather than a sticky blob. It may come straight or it may include small pieces of vegetables or meat. In the Ottoman days it used to be a meal in its own right but in the course of time it has taken a secondary position as a garnish to meat or poultry dishes.

The vertical rotisserie used in the preparation of doner kebab, recognised by many as Turkey's alternative to the hamburger. (Photo: Turkey Tourist Office)

Bread

As national foods, people may associate fish-and-chips with England, paella with Spain, curry with India and chilli con carne with Mexico but those who think *döner kebab* is the Turkish equivalent are mistaken. True, kebab of any kind is on everybody's favourite food list in Turkey but meat is expensive and therefore inaccessible for many people, who are content when they have baked beans and rice with a helping of pickled cucumbers on the side. Otherwise, it is bread with curd cheese, bread with olives, bread with onions, bread with anything. In any case, Turkish cookery involves a lot of stewing with plenty of stock left on the plate, so bread in small pieces is used to sponge up this juice and eaten, ensuring the healthiest part of the meal is not wasted.

The average bread consumption for a family of four is roughly two or three loaves of bread daily. Indeed bread is such an important food item that in the 1994 municipal elections, the candidate from the pro-Islamic Welfare Party won in the capital of the secular republic, Ankara, after he had promised a reduction in the price of bread.

Bread enjoys a sacred status. Children are taught not to leave the table before they finish their bread, the leftovers are never thrown in the bin but given to the poor, and if someone drops a piece of bread accidentally on the ground, it is customary to pick it up, kiss it and then touch the forehead with it, in an act of reverence.

The Turks have no difficulty in adapting to the food of other cultures except when it comes to their bread. This was a source of constant complaint amongst the Turkish migrant workers in Germany, until a clever man started a bakery producing bread in the Turkish way and became a millionaire.

Sweet and Savoury

Traditional Turkish sweets are very sweet indeed. *Baklava*, the most famous, is made of thin pastry leaves, buttered and layered with nuts, and immersed in heavy syrup. As if the amount of sugar they contain is not enough, some of these sweets come with a generous dollop of cream on the top – definitely not for calorie counters.

Among the savoury things, *kısır*, a cold salad made with cracked wheat, tomatoes, parsley, mint, spring onions and hot paprika, needs a special mention as it is both tasty and healthy. Making pickles is another area where the Turks excel with a variety ranging from walnuts to all types of vegetables.

In the patisserie (*pastahane*) one can find the most exquisite sweet cakes alongside the savoury, cheesy, even spicy biscuits and among these, *baton salé*, a biscuit of French origin, should be tried.

DRINKS

Beer and wine exist and are very cheap but the popular alcoholic beverage at the table is *rakı*, which is made of aniseed. Normally a water like liquid, it immediately turns milky white when mixed with water. It is sipped slowly and over a long period of time accompanied by *meze* (hors d'oevres). It is an excellent drink for those who are happy with its unusual taste, and does not lead to a hangover the next day. However, regarding its immediate effects some caution is necessary. As the Turks themselves say, "*Rakı* does not stay in the body as innocently as it does in the bottle," hence the nickname – lion's milk!

Among the non-alcoholic drinks, *ayran* is the popular one. It is made of yoghurt, liquidised with water and cooled with ice cubes, and is especially good on hot summer days.

Water

When you dine in a Turkish restaurant they automatically give you plain water from some celebrated spring. If you prefer alcohol you have to ask for it. The Turks have a fine palate and are able to distinguish differences of taste between one water and another.

Tap water is not safe to drink. The drinking water comes in plastic bottles of various sizes – if only they were easier to open! A more

economical way is to subscribe to the water seller *(sucu)* who brings a large container of water to your house once a week and takes the old one away. The growing significance of fresh water supplies in Istanbul can be seen by the sudden emergence of water stations along many streets, where you can fill your containers with water using a petrol station type pump mechanism, and similarly be charged according to the number of litres you have taken.

While travelling in Turkey you will notice the abundance of fountains by the side of the road. Water continuously pours out of these and one is amazed at the fact that such freezing water gushes out from an earth which is assaulted by the scorching sun. There is no danger in drinking this spring water – it is the gift of mother nature to thirsty travellers.

House guests who ask for water to drink are served a glass sitting on a pretty, embroidered, starched, lacy cloth-covered saucer. The guest only takes the glass, while the hostess waits with the saucer in her hand. Strangers to this custom may hurry the water down to the point of suffocation, but by doing so they will only offend their hostess, who is adopting this servile position as a part of good hospitality.

Tea and Coffee

Many people think that the world famous Turkish coffee is home-grown. This is not true. It is imported, mostly from Latin America. On the other hand, not many people are aware that Turkey is a tea producing country (in the northeast region), for Turkish tea is unknown outside the country's boundaries.

Tea is drunk in tiny, vase-like, transparent glasses and never mixed with milk. If anything, a slice of lemon may accompany it on the saucer alongside two sugar cubes. The glass is small, so people have four or five helpings, one after the other. To indicate that one cannot take any more, the spoon is placed horizontally on top of the glass.

Coffee is made in a special pot with a long handle and comes in a china cup much smaller than those used in Europe. Sugar has to be boiled together with the coffee, so before making it people will ask whether you wish to have it with sugar *(sekerli)* or without *(sade)*.

The texture of the liquid is much stronger than instant or even percolated coffee and the residues sink to the bottom of the cup which, if turned upside down into a saucer, will provide an unexpected source of fun, as someone will no doubt volunteer to read your fortune after a pattern has set inside the cup. The speed with which most Turkish people seem to be able to interpret this pattern is quite bewildering.

DINNER TABLE ETIQUETTE

Table mats are not very much in use in Turkish homes, where the dinner table, like most of the other furniture, is covered with an embroidered or lacy, starched white cloth with matching napkins. In some cases these table cloths are so pretty and valuable (dating back to the Ottoman times and passed down from mother to daughter for generations) that one feels as if one is sitting on a knife-edge for fear of dropping or spilling something on them.

Generally speaking, the seating order at the table does not encourage individuals to socialise with those of the opposite sex, especially if they are married. The couples are seated either together, with the husband next to his wife, or separate, but this time with the wives on one side of the table while the husbands are on the other. The latter seating plan is mocked even by those who practise it as 'The Harem Style' but nonetheless is implemented so as to create different conversational topic territories.

Before starting the meal the host or hostess says, *"Afiyet olsun"* (May it be healthy), to get everybody into action. Similarly, the first sip of the *rakı* or wine is given the go-ahead by the couple entertaining, together with a toast – *"Serefinize"* (To your good honour). It is interesting to note that the Turks drink to the honour, while most other nations drink to the health of their company. This is perhaps a good indication as to how much importance is placed on one's good name and reputation in Turkey. It is good manners to say to the hostess, *"Elinize saglık"* (Health to your hands) in appreciation of the food.

The hostess in a more traditional home does not sit down but serves everybody at the table. This may create a very uncomfortable feeling in a guest but any attempt to make her sit and eat with others is futile, as she will not feel that she is accomplishing her duties as a good hostess unless she serves.

After various *mezes* in small dishes as starters, comes the main course, which is usually meat or poultry served with salad and a starchy food like rice, macaroni or pastry. The second course is invariably one or two cold vegetables cooked in olive oil, or *börek*. Next come the sweets, followed by seasonal fruit. There is no cheese board as cheese is considered within the *meze* category.

With this amount to consume, it is not surprising if one does not have much enthusiasm left for a second helping, but even if you can manage more, it is customary to say no initially. So how will the hostess understand when a no really means no? The guest who is determined not to have any more will have to make his objections most determinedly and put up a gentle fight over his empty plate so that it is not removed for a second helping.

Once the food is finished, the cutlery is left in such a way that the top of the knife is on the right and that of the fork on the left, while they cross one another in the middle of the plate.

It is not impolite to stretch out for items at the table. Why bother other diners if the things are within reach? It is even acceptable to rise from your seat and reach to the other side of the table.

There is no social ban on smoking between courses. In Turkey having a meal can be a very extended occasion and can take longer than most addicts are prepared to wait. As for the hubble-bubble or water pipe, which has been closely associated with Turkey, it is almost an extinct entity, samples of which are more commonly found these days in shops selling antique pieces or souvenirs for tourists.

ENTERTAINMENT PLACES

The Turks love night life, as long as they can afford it. In the large cities, bars and tavernas are plentiful but for the former, some caution is necessary so as to avoid ending up in an unsuitable place with embarrassing consequences. The golden rule is to beware of 'chance' meetings, and never to enter a bar with such an acquaintance, no matter how harmless he may seem. Many a worldly-wise tourist has been fleeced of all of his money by making such false assumptions about the character of his host.

Some nightclubs have only Turkish music and some others Western music, although there are also those which offer a mix. Especially in tourist areas, some nightclubs put belly-dancers on their programme. If you have never experienced this kind of show and you are a male, be prepared to be pulled on to the stage by the dancer, who will ask you to imitate her and make fun of your attempts to do so.

Men on their own are not welcome in some locations and may be turned away from the entrance if the entertainment place accepts 'families' only. This does not mean that you should be married in order to gain entry, it only means you should have a female companion so that you will not look for one once you are inside.

85

Belly dancing remains a popular tourist drawcard and can be seen in many Turkish nightspots. (Photo: Turkish Tourist Office)

RESTAURANTS

Restaurants cover almost all cuisines and which one to choose depends on what you want to try and how much you are prepared to pay. Of course all cities have a list of their best restaurants but no other city can take pride in beating Istanbul in quality and quantity. Among those worth mentioning are the Galata Tower restaurant for lovers of European cuisine, Pandelli in Eminönü and Abdullah Efendi in Emirgan (both excellent for Turkish food), Osmanlı Mutfagı next to the Kaariye Mosque (for authentic Ottoman food) and Rejans in Galatasaray (for Russian cuisine). Hacı Abdullah in Beyoglu is also famous for its Turkish dishes and has on display an incredibly rich selection of jars with different pickles, jams and marmalades which is a joy to see. People who like the Greek style tavern will enjoy the atmosphere in Despina in Kurtulus. There is a good Chinese restaurant in the Istanbul Hilton and those looking for Byzantium decor should try Sarnıç.

Restaurants do not normally display their price range outside the door, so most Turks choose one either on recommendation or prior experience or by the looks of the entrance. Too posh an entrance usually means too high a figure on the bill and neither is a guarantee for the quality of food.

In Turkey women have entered most professional areas, from the police force to the prime ministry, but one of the few jobs which they have not developed an interest in is waitressing (another is driving taxis). Gender is also a factor in deciding who orders and pays in restaurants. Among male diners, the one who has invited the other gets the bill, but when it comes to a woman, there is only one rule in force: they cannot be the payers in restaurants if there is male company present. Why? Need you ask – manliness is not dead yet!

WHAT TO WEAR

There will always be those overdressed for any occasion, but in general, the rules for choosing the right kind of clothes in Turkey are no different from those observed in most European countries. However, a word of caution may be helpful here – do not wear shorts on the day you are visiting mosques. Although most religious places are equipped with 'decent' spare clothes, which the officials will force on you at the entrance should the need arise, there is a constant danger of a shortage and consequently of female visitors ending up with oversized pairs of trousers, or males with long, pretty frocks!

Chapter Five

OUT OF DOORS

A TYPICAL TURKISH STREET

A Turkish street is a place bubbling with vitality. Exciting as well as surprising, it is a scene of events with minute details which combine to give the authentic character to the whole.

In the early hours of the day a horse-drawn cart carrying fresh fruit and vegetables will try to squeeze through the narrow alley created by the latest models of Mercedes cars, hooded to protect them from the invasive dust, and parked on either side of the road in front of rows of houses. The buildings themselves are a mishmash, some dilapidated houses with patches where the whitewash has long been stripped off, others well maintained tower blocks of modern, luxurious flats, sometimes higher than the minaret of the local mosque.

Little girls, arm-in-arm, giggling and looking like newly blossomed white lilies with huge ribbons perched on their heads, will hurry past the shopkeepers who sit on chairs in front of their shops, with worry beads in their hands to occupy them until a customer walks in. Little boys break a twig each while passing, only to throw it into the communal waste bin a few yards further on. A *simitçi* boy (a seller of rings of crisp bread sprinkled with sesame seeds), his shaven head shining under the early beams of the sun, will do his best business of the day, while other children in their blue uniforms and white collars sing the national anthem in the garden of the district school, gathered around the dark bronze bust of Atatürk, which looks like the work of their art teacher rather than of a commissioned sculptor.

The caretakers of blocks of flats (the Turks call them apartments) will ignore one another lest they forget the memorised list of items they are supposed to carry back to the flats, and walk in haste to the corner shops with their huge basket carriers. A man at the corner will be looking through a newspaper while his shoes are taken care of by a shoeshine boy. The young coffee-house apprentice will carry in his brass tray, jingling glasses of tea, to be distributed to different shop keepers.

People will hop in and out of taxis, cars, minibuses, buses – all hooting their horns to scare other drivers off, so that they will have the right of way. Street vendors, uniformed soldiers, beggars, retired men on their daily stroll, stray cats and dogs, will all appear in good time. The air will buzz with radio music of all types.

A woman who is hanging her washing out on her back balcony will shout at her neighbour upstairs to look down first before shaking the bread-crumbs out of her table cloth, still feeling relieved that at least she is not shaking out her carpet. The home-help in baggy trousers on the top floor will step onto the sill to clean the outside of the windows, bringing the spectators' hearts into their mouths. Another woman will lift bread in a basket tied to a rope and then let it down from her window to the ground.

In the afternoon the children will play hide-and-seek, hopscotch or football in the street and jump around the heaps of sand, timber and brick on the construction sites of which every street has one or more, at all times. Ladies of leisure, anxious not to damage their high heels between the cobbled stones, will hurry to their 'coon king' card parties. A man in a bathrobe will call down from his balcony to the caretaker to check why the water has stopped all of a sudden. A cortège of campaign cars, covered with banners and flags, will pass, emitting loud music from the speakers and millions of small papers from the windows. A man will jump out of one of the cars to stick a poster on the wall of a deserted building, which is thick with hundreds of posters already stuck there, ranging from advertisements for nightclub singers to those for washing powders.

A porter who is bent under a high pile of crates will leave his load in front of the greengrocer and wait for his meagre pay. When he receives it, he will kiss the bank-note and brush it against his brow, in gratitude to God. A lorry-driver will park his vehicle in the middle of the road and disappear into the coffee-house for a quick round of backgammon, oblivious of the queue of cars forming outside and of the anger of their drivers.

As cooking smells overpower those of the exhaust fumes, the homecoming husbands will buy a watermelon or two from the vendor who has piled up his goods by the side of the road. The streets, which are normally quiet by nine o'clock in winter, will liven up again in the hot season after dinner. Young people will congregate at street corners to show off their clothing: Nike, Adidas, Levi's, Wrangler, Benetton, and whatever other labels are currently in fashion. Modest women, their hair imprisoned under headscarves, will sit on their doorsteps and talk, while groups of young men stroll about aimlessly, leaving a trail of sunflower seed husks behind them. Voices of protest from the television addicts will simultaneously travel into the street from the open balcony doors bemoaning the temporary local power cut, almost as if orchestrated by a magic wand.

After midnight, the crowds will gradually disappear, until finally all that can be heard is the continuous chirruping of the crickets in the summer and the occasional barks of the stray dogs in winter.

STREET VENDORS

In the Ottoman times, the streets were allocated to shops selling the same type of goods or giving the same kind of service. The names of some of these have survived, especially in Istanbul, where you will find, for instance, *Kazancılar Yokusu* (The Slope of Cauldron-makers), *Kuyumcular Çarsısı* (The Market of Jewellers), *Topçular Caddesi* (The Street of Artillerymen) and *Vezneciler* (The District of Cashiers). These days they are not specific to one profession alone and accommodate shops and offices of all kinds. What is more, in present day Turkey trade does not have to be confined to a fixed location. Any spot has trade potential as long as the municipal police are not around the corner. Indeed, street vendors who carry and promote various forms of merchandise in various forms and styles are a common sight and sound in Turkish streets.

To be a good street vendor you not only need the agility to make yourself and your goods disappear immediately should the need arise; but also a good voice to sing out the cries to attract the attention of the prime customers, that is to say, the housewives. With the development of new technology, vans equipped with siren systems have come on the scene too but this has not killed off the tradition of street vendors who rely on their vocal chords for the promotion of their goods. From the early hours of the morning until nightfall, the streets echo with different voices at different pitches and different intervals.

The usual goods sold by itinerant traders are nuts and seeds, boiled, grilled or popped corn, roasted chestnuts, ice-cream, toffee-apples, sweets, yoghurt, various savoury pastries filled with meat or

91

Almost anything can be bought from the street vendors. Here a seller of bird-seed offers the chance to feed the city's pigeons. (Photo: Turkish Tourist Office)

cheese, newspapers, lottery tickets, plastic kitchen ware, fresh flowers, milk, drinks made of yoghurt *(ayran)*, lemonade *(limonata)*, fermented millet *(boza)*, and even plain drinking water.

Most of these wandering salesmen do not have a fixed route but there are also others who come to the same spot, at the same time, on the same day every week. Vegetable and fruit sellers, transporting their goods in horse-drawn carts, are usually of this type. Then there are others who bring their trade literally to your doorstep. Women selling embroidered bed-linen, tablecloths, towels and underwear for your daughter's bottom drawer fall into this category. Similarly, gypsies come to tell you your fortune, and the junkmen come in case you have things to discard. You may even find a beggar outside your door, showing you a tattered piece of paper, supposed to be a doctor's prescription, or carrying a baby in her arms. People get rid of the last type of visitor by saying, *"Allah versin"* (May God give you) and then closing the door. Of course, there is no logic in this because if God had given her what she needed, she would not be at your door begging, but after all, wishing someone well before slamming the door in her face may be better than doing the same thing without any words.

STREET ANIMALS

The streets are full of stray cats and dogs, and as they do not get the necessary injections, one should be very wary when handling them, or better still, not handle them at all. In open air restaurants especially, these animals come and sit next to your table, fixing their eyes on whatever you are eating and waiting for you to throw half of your food on the ground for their consumption.

TRAFFIC

A Swiss racing driver made a very interesting remark about the traffic in Turkey and Turkish drivers. He said driving in Switzerland was too dull because one knows or at least expects that everybody will act according to the laws. In Turkey, in contrast, driving is an experience full of surprises. "People come from the right and the left, they barge in from the back or suddenly come to a stop, right in front of you. There is no way that you can predict what will happen next. You must always be on your toes, ready to react when the need arises. Some may call this dangerous but I call it exciting."

No matter how you look at it, the fact remains that Turkey is among the countries with the highest rate of road accidents. There has been a campaign going on for several years now to warn the drivers not to let the 'traffic monster' in them take over their conscience, but with little, if any, effect. A sign I saw at a repair garage on a highway presented the same message more effectively: **We do not have the spare parts for your life, so drive with care.** It was a shame that its readership consisted only of the limited number of motorists who

93

happened to come that way. The truth of the matter is that the traffic fines are too low to intimidate and generous traffic wardens may even waive them.

At a conference, an ex-British Ambassador started his speech with a story of his first day in Turkey. Apparently he drove to Turkey so as to see more of the country on the way to Ankara but, after crossing the border at Kapıkule, he was in haste to reach Istanbul before nightfall and put his foot down on the accelerator. The next thing he knew, a traffic policeman was catching up with him and forcing him to stop. He handed over his passport and driving licence as requested. The official asked him whether he knew that the fine for speeding was 500,000 lira. He said he did not know but as he was the new British Ambassador to Ankara, no doubt he would learn these things in time. The eyes of the policeman opened wide in amazement. He said, "The new British Ambassador? Have I stopped the new British Ambassador? What will people think of me and my hospitality! I beg your pardon, sir. The fine for you is 50,000 lira."

Driving in Turkey, one gets the impression that everybody is in the utmost hurry, as if in a case of emergency. Every driver holds the steering wheel with thumbs poised, ready to hoot the horn. There are various messages passed on by the way one hoots. The most frequently used one is a short, abrupt touch to give out a brief warning sound. This is equivalent to saying, "I am behind you, or next to you, so watch out!" The same may also mean, "Thank you." Then, there is a long, stubborn pressing on the horn, to reprimand or reproach. This comes when the other driver thinks you have abused his rights. You may not agree with his judgement and respond in exactly the same way. With all these warnings and reprimands, driving becomes a very noisy exercise indeed.

In most cities traffic consists of all possible forms of transport, apart from an ox-cart. Among this rich variety the absence of bicycles is noticeable – bikes are thought to be for children only and are more common in summer resorts than in the bustling city centres. Not counting the symbolic underground car in Istanbul, called *tünel* (the tunnel), which is amazing to watch when it appears as if emerging from the centre of the earth, neither in Istanbul nor in Ankara is there an underground network yet, although construction in both locations is in progress. At present everybody is above ground and both cities appear to be over populated. This, of course, is true, especially in the case of Istanbul, which recorded a population of nearly 12 million in the last census, but with a proper rail system life will be easier for commuters.

Pedestrians

Crossing from one side of the street to the other requires courage, especially in the city centres. The Turks themselves seem to have acquired the art of crossing the road, even when the traffic is flowing but the inexperienced stranger is advised not to make a solo attempt but to venture out only in the shelter of the locals. For mortal

Westerners it is often difficult to get used to the close city traffic that one finds, especially in Istanbul. Turkish grandmothers and little children will nonchalantly walk within inches of fast, passing traffic while foreigners will hurriedly seek the safety of the high pavements. As for the times right after the Cup final or when a Turkish football team has won a match overseas, it is best for any pedestrian, Turk or otherwise, to stay indoors for his or her peace of mind.

If you think you have lost your way, do not hesitate to ask for assistance. The Turks are very helpful; they may even go out of their way to take you to your destination themselves.

Taxis

Taxi fares are very cheap in Turkey compared to most other countries. You can stop a taxi by raising your arm. Their bright yellow colour is easy to recognise. Taxis charge by the meter but there is a small surcharge for unsociable hours. Deception is not common but make sure that the driver knows where he is taking you.

BUSES

While taxis are cheap in Turkey, the buses are even cheaper but it is a job to get on and off them, especially during rush hours when they are packed with people. If you are a frequent user, get a season ticket.

Dolmus

This is a minibus operating on a prescribed route in the crowded cities, picking up and setting down passengers at any point en route. As they are more convenient than public buses and cheaper than taxis, they are very popular. The word *dolmus* means "full" and they usually are. However, some *dolmus* drivers bring their vehicle to the bursting point by taking more passengers than they are allowed to and nobody objects to this. Especially during the rush hours, people are happier to travel in such conditions than to wait for the next available *dolmus*.

Traffic wardens, on the other hand, are not so lenient but they too can be pacified by ingenuity. Hasan Pulur, a famous columnist, once wrote about his experience in one of these minibuses. Apparently after the last passenger was squeezed in, the driver saw a traffic warden in the distance. He immediately produced a small drum from under his seat, passed it to the passenger sitting behind him and begged, "Go on, brothers, sing a song as if we were a wedding party." The passengers, who were complete strangers to one another, were astounded at this request but nonetheless went along with it. While one passenger played on the drum, the others with smiling faces, sang a popular song at the tops of their voices, until they passed by the warden who, as expected, mistook them for the groom's relatives and refrained from being a kill-joy to the overcrowded but innocent merrymakers.

It should perhaps be mentioned in passing that Turkish *dolmus* drivers seem to be the only human beings capable of doing six things at the same time: chatting to fellow passengers, cleaning the windscreen, waving at friends along the route, taking passengers' fares, scanning the roads for passengers wishing to board, and of course, looking at the road ahead!

Intercity Coaches

This is the most economical way to travel long distances. There are plenty of coach companies to choose from and at any coach station representatives of these will rush to prospective customers to attract them to the merits of their services. Rather than going for the most persuasive of these representatives, it is best to ask some friends to find out which are the most reliable companies beforehand. Good companies offer better services in deluxe coaches, and the services may include a television set on board, a rest break every now and then at comfortable teahouses, free drinks and biscuits, and a new driver every few hours. The last is especially important as some coach companies use drivers to the point of exhaustion, leaving the fate of their passengers to Allah, as the banners on the coaches – *Allah büyüktür* (God is great) *Allahn dedigi olur* (Whatever will be will be) *Masallah* (May God protect) – usually demonstrate.

Most coach drivers are lovers of Arabesque music and are in the habit of listening to it at full volume. Of course they turn it down each time they are reprimanded by passengers who do not appreciate the same type of music, only to increase it gradually until the next warning comes.

There is no ban on smoking in these coaches but you can easily change your seat so as to be with fellow non-smokers. Smokers are used to this and no offence will be taken.

Public toilets on the highways are not properly subsidised and therefore lack on the basic requirements and cleaning. Turks who travel usually carry a bar of soap, toilet tissue and even a bottle of eau-de-cologne to sterilise their hands with, knowing the conditions of these lavatories. In addition to such items, perhaps having an alarm whistle might also come in handy in case one locks oneself in a closet – they are renowned for their dodgy locks.

For those who like watching the scenery from a window, intercity journeys offer a pleasant variety especially along the coastline. Additionally, passengers are informed of all the hotels, restaurants, and places of interest by an army of metal billboards erected by the side of the road, starting miles before the boundaries of any city.

Intercity coaches can stop anywhere if someone on board wants to get off or the driver sees a prospective passenger on the way. In the rest of the world the passenger is on the look out for a coach but in Turkey the coach is on the look out for a passenger.

TRAINS

Apart from the 'Blue Train' which is in service between Ankara and Istanbul, there are no fast trains operating in Turkey but trains have the advantage of being the safest form of travel.

Turkish rail abolished the class system years ago but those who seek luxury will be pleasantly surprised by the restaurant car, which can compete with a first class restaurant with its starched, white tablecloths, extensive menus and waiters in uniform.

SHOPPING

Turkey is a shopper's paradise. The big shops and department stores in the city centres are open until 6:00 p.m. but smaller shops in residential areas do not close until ten o'clock in the evening or later. As for those in seaside resort towns, trading goes on until the early hours of the morning.

Shop assistants are quick, helpful and friendly. They talk to all passers-by and invite them to come and view the goods inside the shop. People who are not used to such treatment may find this alienating but those who are too polite to say no to the invitation and walk into the shop will tell you otherwise. It is not uncommon to end up sipping tea with the shop assistants and conversing with them as if they were your bosom friends, despite the fact that no transaction has taken or is likely to take place.

First time visitors to the country will be surprised to find so many common names on the shops – Metro, Tesco, Migros, Lindt, Ralph Lauren, Printemps, Chemignon, Maxmara, Equipment, Rolex, Cartier, etc. Others will know that Turkey is now an open market and can import everything from Cardin's latest creations to Tupperware pieces. However, as the popular version of the poet's words has it, all that glitters is not gold, so those who come across a 'Rolex' watch bearing a price tag for the equivalent of US$8.00 should not rub their eyes in disbelief, the item is probably home produced and will work only as long as any other watch of that value.

Packaging is a form of art which every shop keeper learns and there cannot be many countries where patisserie goods, for example, are wrapped up or flower arrangements presented in a more artistic way. Likewise, the gift wrapping paper and ribbons are of excellent quality and if bought in quantity may save one considerable sums from the next Christmas packaging funds.

The Turks hate small change. In a country where the inflation rate has been in three figures for some time, dealing with pence and dimes is thought to be a stupid waste of time. For this reason, rather than searching for the small coins in their drawers, the shopkeepers thrust a bubble gum or a box of matches at you, as your change. Of course, this is also a good way for them to trade in less worthy items. Most customers are content with this transaction but an Irish tourist I met in Marmaris complained bitterly: "If it were only once, I wouldn't have minded," she said, "but in two weeks all this change adds up to a considerable sum and I am sick and tired of carrying all these wretched boxes of matches in my bag!" She was genuinely distressed so I dared not suggest that she should try to buy her next loaf of bread with the matches.

Finally, the bazaars. People who think there is only one bazaar in Turkey, the famous Covered Bazaar in Istanbul, are mistaken. Every city, even every district, has a bazaar but these bazaars are set up only once a week, on a certain day. The bazaars are popular because the producers sell their goods without the involvement of a middleman so everything is cheaper than it would be in the shops – sometimes half the price. Some are only for vegetables and fruit but there are also major bazaars where a vast range is on sale, from textiles to plastic goods, from spices to bric-a-brac.

Carpets

Turkish carpets are famous worldwide for their quality. The oldest known carpet making centre in history is said to be Konya. Marco Polo mentions the workshops in this city, under the patronage of the Seljuk Sultans during the 13th century. Since then, other areas, such as Kula, Bergama and Hereke in the west, Kayseri and Isparta in Central Anatolia and Kars in the east have flourished as important centres for hand-woven carpets. Today, near Istanbul, there are also factories whose products compete with the real thing and sell in numbers as large, not because of their quality but because of their price. Large cities and tourist resorts are under invasion by carpet shops but the same goods can be bought for half the price or even less on the production sites.

Carpet making is a form of art in its own right and can be studied at university level in Turkey. The regional differences are reflected in the choice of patterns, colour, materials and knotting.

Some are made of cotton and some of pure silk but the most revered are those made of wool. To protect their wool carpets from moths, the Turks usually roll them up in the summer with plenty of moth-repelling naphthalene crystals and store them away in dark rooms.

While patterns range from small, flowery arrangements to large geometric shapes, depending on which region the carpet comes from, the colours too show a variety from pale, pastel shades to rich, earthy tones, due to different vegetable dyes and dying techniques. In the old times, these techniques were kept within the same region or even the same family, as a carefully guarded trade secret, to eliminate competition from rival manufacturers.

Not only do the patterns sometimes tell a story, the colours used also have a meaning. Red is a dominant colour in Turkish carpets, expressing wealth, happiness and joy. Green has heavenly connotations. Yellow is to ward off evil and blue signifies grandeur and nobility.

What is specific to Turkish carpets is the form of weaving. Whereas Afghan or Persian carpets, for instance, are single-knotted, the Turkish ones are made of double-knotting. The difference may not be obvious to the naked eye but it is a fact that double-knotting makes a carpet stronger, firmer and more durable. This is why the Turk calls his carpet *evladiyelik* (for the child), meaning it is to be left to the next generation.

The fine quality and intricate designs of Turkish carpets have made them keenly sought the world over. Caution should be exercised, however, to ensure authenticity; be aware also of the regulations which govern the export of antique items. (Photo: Turkish Tourist Office)

One point to be borne in mind is that taking an antique carpet, more than 60-years-old, out of Turkey is a punishable act and if one is not certain about the age of a carpet, expert advice should be sought, even if it means travelling to another city with the carpet. To stay awake, as the Turks say, is better than having nightmares.

It is always best, if possible, to take a Turkish friend with you when purchasing a carpet – especially if you intend to send it overseas. Though a relatively rare occurrence, it has been known for an unsuspecting tourist to unroll a completely different carpet in England from that chosen in the carpet shop in Turkey.

Leather Goods

Leather is a good buy, in the form of fashionable clothing, bags and footwear and is perhaps the cheapest one can find in Europe. It will be even more so if you go directly to the manufacturer rather than buying the items in upmarket leather shops. Caution is necessary on several points though. Make sure that the material has been properly treated (if it smells, do not touch it because this smell will stay with it forever), coloured effectively and sewn firmly.

Jewellery

Whether from an urban or pastoral background, the Turks invest their money in jewellery, especially gold jewellery, more than anything else. While city women favour bracelets and rings with precious stones, most women from rural areas go for plain gold earrings and thin, gold bracelets. A man's wealth is said to be valued by the number of gold bracelets his wife wears. These slim bracelets are bought one after the other at times of prosperity only to be sold one by one when hardship strikes the family. In view of the demand for their products, jewellers have to be inventive and introduce fashionable artifacts to compete with one another. The outcome is very innovative but sometimes excessively showy pieces of jewellery. Most pieces are of 18 carat, although 22 carat goods are also easy to come by.

Towels

It is no coincidence that towels are of the highest quality in a country which is famous for its baths. The best towels used to come from Bursa, also renowned for its natural hot springs, but these days the southern region also claims expertise in this area. In the past a girl's dowry was judged by the embroidered border on her towels. Golden thread embroidery meant wealth, while modesty was evident in the silk or cotton embroidered ones. The same tradition is still carried on in the small guest towels one can buy today, but with one difference. Those in the old days were handmade, while the modern products are machine sewn. It is a relief, however, that the fluffy, soft quality of the famous Ottoman towels has been maintained, if not bettered, in an age of progress in textiles.

Cigarettes

Turkey grows its own tobacco, which is well known for its quality worldwide, but the number of smokers in Turkey is so high that it can consume all its crop internally rather than exporting it. Apart from sporadic attempts to create an anti-smoking movement, no systematic campaign has taken place there and people are not used to seeing non-smoking signs in public places.

When Turkish Airlines banned smoking on their domestic flights, it created an outcry. Ask your host whether smoking is allowed in his house and he will look at you in as much amazement as if you had asked for permission to breathe. Consequently, cigarettes, Turkish or foreign made (mostly American), are on sale everywhere at a price much lower than in other

European countries. And of course, the chances of cigarette buyers getting their small change in the form of boxes of matches are higher than for anybody else.

Turkish Delight

Made with cornstarch and sugar syrup, cubes of genuine Turkish delight are of a chewing-gum consistency and have not even a distant cousin's relationship with the chocolatey, caramel, creamy pieces you may be familiar with. The sticky surface is usually tempered with powdered sugar. Some come with almond and pistachio nuts inside. Further variation is possible in the flavour, like having a minty or lemony taste, but the most unusual and perhaps the most exquisite version is the one flavoured with rose water.

Turkish delight is a popular going away present. People will come for miles just to see you for a few minutes at the railway station and discreetly deposit a box of Turkish delight in your baggage, with the usual, "It is not worthy of you but ...."

Bargaining

It is important for a visitor to Turkey to have some idea of the techniques of bargaining, because without this knowledge one probably pays more for anything which has no price tag than it is worth. Now, do not get overanxious and think that you will be cheated every time you open your purse. In Turkey, starting from a high price is one of the rules of trading and every buyer knows this. It is the same mutual knowledge which makes the seller's price offer legitimate. What happens is that the seller starts from the highest extreme and the buyer from the lowest and only after a tug-of-war do they meet in the middle, which is more or less the right price of the goods. If the furthest each can go does not reach the point of convergence, then the whole effort becomes abortive. The golden rule, however, is not to get involved in this activity if you have no intention of buying.

Telling the sales assistant that you do not want a receipt *(fis)* can often result in a quick drop in the price. Another way is to offer attractive prospects for future transactions, as Holly Chase points out in *Turkish Tapestry*:

> (At) Samanpazarı (a market place on the outskirts of Ankara) merchants are eager to ensure repeat trade. Rather than overcharge a one-time customer, a seller is more likely to offer an especially attractive first-time price. They say, *"Siftah senden, bereket Allah'tan,"* which can be loosely translated as, "A sale to you brings blessings from God." And the goodwill continues should a customer return or recommend the shop to a friend. Just as the seller tempts the buyer back, the buyer piques the interest of the seller by asking for a better price if he buys two or more of something. A discount must benefit both parties, or it will never be given. An astute shopper quickly learns that even in a relaxed environment where merchants seem to have endless hours to spend bargaining, time is valued. In this bazaar, any browser who offers an insulting quarter of the asking price is immediately recognised as an idle time-waster scarcely worth a goodbye.

No doubt, the mastery of bargaining can only be obtained through experience; one has to pluck up courage and go out and try it, once, and then twice, and then at each opportunity. The more you do it, the better you will become. Who knows, there is even the possibility that you may outwit the most experienced trader.

Souvenir Shopping

Like most souvenir shops in any other country, those in Turkey are full of good-for-nothing, jingle-jangle and poor quality items which are produced simply to obtain the last few bank-notes that a tourist is trying to get rid of before he or she leaves for home. On offer are

Souvenir sellers specialise in the more clichéd aspects of Turkish culture but can be ideal places to hone your bargaining skills while searching for gifts and mementos. (Photo: Turkish Tourist Office)

colourful, satin slippers with upturned pointed ends, blue eye beads of all forms and shapes, brass ornaments, painted and lacquered wooden spoons, green and beige marble ashtrays and vases, miniature hubble-bubbles, copper wall plates, and lucky-charm sets of seven elephants adorned with mini-bells, to name but a few items. Take your pick depending on how heavy your purse still feels or how much bartering skill you have acquired so far.

Chapter Six

CULTURE AND LEISURE

THE ARTS

In aesthetic matters Turkish taste is an amalgamation of their Central Asian inheritance, the impact of the Byzantines and the religion they adopted after their migration to the West. Combined with this is their struggle for the last two hundred years to join the European clan and hence their readiness to follow Western artistic trends, most readily seen in late 19th century literature. These factors are to be found in combination in all the fine arts, although in different proportions, depending on the form.

Theatre

As in all Asiatic cultures, the traditional Turkish theatre is a total entity containing music, dance, theatrical art and acrobatics. The object is to produce laughter or a sensuous pleasure in the spectator. This applies to shadow theatre as much as to the improvised farce by live actors *(ortaoyunu)*, the Turkish version of commedia dell'arte, which is a unique dramatic form not existing in other Islamic countries. When Western ideas started infiltrating the Turkish dramatic arts in the 19th century, Italian canto and French chansonette also found a firm place here, as people loved actresses singing, dancing and making appropriate gestures to mime the words of the song at the same time. Later on, interest grew in the world classics, and in the years to come audiences had this thirst quenched by everything from Sophocles to Strindberg, from Shakespeare to Pirandello and from Moliére to Gorki. The most popular drama form, however, is the cabaret, a combination of music, dance and farce interwoven in a story.

Cinema

Since 1914, when the first Turkish film was made, the film industry in Turkey has not shown a very healthy rate of growth. Its infancy coincided with the World Wars and the ensuing economic crises. The prime time for Yesilçam (Turkey's Hollywood) was in the fifties and sixties. Despite the fact that the majority of films made during this period were based on escapist stories, like the rich girl marrying the poor boy or vice versa, and that they were produced under technologically deprived circumstances, there was a constant flow to the cinemas. This period is most memorable for the open air cinemas to which people went on hot summer evenings, with bags full of enough sunflower seeds to last them throughout the double feature. This was followed by a period when the film makers decided to appeal to the more educated spectator at the expense of alienating the faithful crowds.

In the 1970s the film industry went from bad to worse. To save the dying patient, in the 1980s the government allowed the American companies to move into Turkey with their off-shore media projects, thinking that they would be bringing not only their films but also their studios to inject ideas, practical experience and income into the national film industry. Instead, the American giants walked in to monopolise the distribution network. Today the newspapers are full of film advertisements commissioned by Warner Brothers, UPI, Standard and the like, who take all their earnings out of Turkey in a package called the royalties, without even paying tax, let alone creating studios to generate life saving income for their Turkish counterparts. In 1989, out of the 222 films which were shown in the cinemas, 210 were of foreign origin.

Today the life saver for the Turkish film industry is the rope thrown by the private television channels. Everybody knows that long lasting survival depends on the emergence of indigenous producers who can produce films better than the Americans do, but waiting for them is like waiting for 'Godot.'

DANCE

If belly dancing is the only dance form you associate with Turkey, you must prepare yourself for a surprise. To start with, belly dancing was not originally Turkish (or Middle Eastern for that matter) but Spanish, and was imported through the Jewish emigration from Spain to Turkey in the late 15th century. Have you heard of the Whirling Dervishes who come from Turkey and dance for the love of God? Did you know that the largest European out-of-doors disco is in Bodrum, a tourist resort on the Aegean coast? Were you aware that there is a school of ballet in Ankara, set up as part of the State Conservatory of Music and Drama, and its first students in 1947 were trained by Dame Ninette de Valois, the well-known choreographer and founder of the British Royal Ballet? There is a lot of dancing going on in the Turkish lands and most of it has little to do with the belly.

Not all Turkish dancing is done with the belly, as this performance of Çesmebas by the Ankara State Ballet shows. (Photo: Turkish Tourist Office)

Social Dancing

Islam discourages music and dancing. Visitors to urban parts of Turkey in the present time, however, will witness anything but a religiously suppressed nation in terms of songs and dance.

An English friend who teaches at a language centre in Istanbul once recounted a story. He said that they had organised a trip to a small Black Sea resort, hiring two coaches in order to take about 120 students. However, they had not bargained with the weather, which for May was distinctly unseasonal, raining torrentially all day. Nevertheless, the students spent the entire journey there and back dancing in the aisles of the coaches and having a wonderful time. In fact, weather which would probably have dampened the spirits of any other nationality on earth did not even seem to register to the Turks at all. If they have their music, why do they need any sun? Similarly, with the slightest chance of an entertainment the Turkish genie is let loose and no religious power can force it to go back into its bottle.

111

Sacred Dancing

In the pre-migration days in Central Asia, the Turkish people believed in Shamanism in which dancing was a means of obtaining a super-natural state. After their conversion to Islam and despite the fact that Islam was waging a war against dancing, the Turks continued with their tradition only to attach a different meaning to it, a divine meaning in which dancing became a movement to symbolise ecstasy in reunion with God. From this sprang various monastic Dervish orders. One of these was the Mevlevi Order.

The Mevlevi Dervishes, or Whirling Dervishes as we call them in English, still practise their ceremonies in Konya where the order was first established in the 13th century by the great Turkish poet and mystic Mevlana Celaleddin Rumi. They perform for tourists and interested Turks once a year in their assembly hall.

Their dancing order is similar to the planetary system; they move round in an orbit for hours, accompanied by mystic music, in an ecstasy of spiritual love and communion with the Eternal. One arm is up in the air while the other arm points down which means that they reach God with one hand and pass the love they have received from Him to the earth with the other. They wear long, conical shaped hats and white robes. It is extremely impressive to watch the dervishes in performance, whirling for hours on end, the white skirts of their robes undulating gracefully.

Folk Dancing

Islam's puritanical attitude towards dancing may have affected some urban people in the past, but it had little effect upon the Turkish villagers, who retained their ethnic unity and their distinctive charac-ter along with their dancing. This was primarily due to the fact that the villages had been cut off from the rest of the world for centuries and as a result, village people were not easy prey for the orthodox Muslims of urban education. They danced, almost always as a group and not solo, on a variety of occasions like birth, puberty, circumcision,

A Whirling Dervish: their sacred dancing, lasting for hours, allows them to achieve a state of spiritual ecstasy. (Photo: Turkish Tourist Office)

marriage, return from military service and release from prison. There are also dances which are associated with holidays, fairs, seasonal festivals and ceremonies.

The isolation of the villages is also the reason we cannot talk about a typical Turkish folk dance. Each region has its own folk dances, quite distinct from the others. Western Turkey is characterised by *zeybek dansı*. The dancers move in a circle as if testing the ground and then touch on the ground with one knee. They hold their arms at their sides first, bringing them to shoulder level later on and snapping their fingers at the same time. It is a solemn dance performed by male dancers only.

Halay dansı is associated with Central Anatolia. The dancers stand in a line or in a semi-circle, holding each other's hands or shoulders. One dancer acts as the leader by regulating the steps and moving the line in the direction he or she chooses. Another dance which comes from the same area is the *kasık oyunu* (the spoon dance) in which the dancers carry a pair of wooden spoons in each hand, and click them as the Spanish click castanets.

Horon dansı comes from Northern Turkey and the Black Sea coast. It consists of alert, tense, shivering movements and the trembling of the entire body from head to foot, like a fish out of water. This is quite appropriate because the inhabitants of this area are mostly fishermen or sailors by profession.

The most romantic folk dance is *çayda çıra dansı* (the dance of fire-lighters in the field) of Southern Turkey, performed by women only, with each dancer carrying a lighted candle in a tray. This dance is usually performed in a girl's house the night before her marriage to bless her future life.

MUSIC

Aaron Hill, an 18th century traveller, wrote: "No one can travel half a day in the Turkish territories but he shall see a grave, long-bearded Musulman sitting cross-legg'd under some large oak, or shady cypress, pleasing his conceit with melancholy ditties, to the strum-strum musick of his thrum'd ghittar, while his poor horse is turn'd to graze about the field, and seeks the pleasure of a more substantial entertainment."

The melancholy ditties are not everybody's cup of tea but there are those who appreciate the delicacies of Turkish music. The Hungarian composer, Béla Bartok, for instance, disclosed that Turkish folk music was the richest he had known. Rich but buried in anonymity –

for centuries, the minstrels have wandered from place to place with nothing but their *saz,* a three stringed instrument with a slender handle, and sung improvised songs at each gathering they happened to chance upon.

Types of Music

Classical Turkish music is an educated and conscious type of music, arranged according to set rules. This was the music listened to in the Ottoman palace and large towns. Among the accompanying instruments is the *ud* which the crusaders must have brought back home as "lude" – eventually, the lute – and which, like divans, tulips, cherries and Angora wool is of Turkish heritage.

Young Turks mostly listen to Turkish pop music, oriental in flavour but European in tempo and instruments. Especially in summer, low-pitched, almost masculine female voices on tape, singing with great fervour, will bombard you from all directions, whether you are in the market, in a restaurant, on a bus, or travelling in a passenger boat in Istanbul. In winter, the concrete on the road will tremble each time a young driver passes by in a car throbbing with the beat of Turkish pop music.

The *Mehter* music, played by the Janisseries in the Ottoman times, is kept alive these days only in remembrance of the country's glorious past. The *mehter* band of 66 instruments, including gigantic drums on special carts, headed the Turkish armies on the march in those days, drumming up encouragement to its followers and fear in the hearts of their foes.

I once overheard a silly conversation amongst a group of language students in England who were discussing at a lunch table whether Eastern or Western music was better. A student whose nationality I did not know, but whose blinkers were apparently wide enough to take in only the European perspective and nothing else, said to a Turkish student: "We have Haydn and Mozart and Beethoven, to name but a few. Who do you have?" The Turk was obviously at a loss to find a name or names to counterbalance the prestigious list quoted. Possibly he did not know or could not remember that the best examples of Turkish music are anonymous anyway, and that the Turkish *mehter* music was good enough to influence Haydn's *Military Symphony*, Mozart's *Turkish March*, *Turkish Violin Concerto*, and *The Abduction from the Seraglio* and Beethoven's Ninth Symphony.

ARCHITECTURE

In Central Asia the Turks lived in dome like tents or in sun-dried brick shelters. They brought their architectural taste with them when they came to make their home in Anatolia. First was the Seljuk period when buildings were constructed for their purpose rather than for their splendour. The solid, austere exterior gives no indication as to what beauties it conceals inside. The silk route during this period was dotted with brick *caravanserais* (inns for passengers) which can provide today an interesting trail for those who wish to follow in the footsteps of the ancient traders.

Turkish architecture began to attain a more aesthetic character both internally and externally in the Ottoman period with impressive palaces, mosques, mausoleums, *medreses* (educational settings), baths, covered bazaars, and fountains. The stocky Seljuk style was replaced by the slender, more curved, more complicated Ottoman outline, revealing from the outside what it covers underneath.

Mosques

The first domed mosque, the first tiled minaret, the first engraved marble niche, the first Ottoman-style mausoleum and *medrese* as well as the first T-shaped buildings are all in Iznik, which also happens to be the first Ottoman capital. In time, mosques were built with more than one dome and one minaret. Two domes became four, then six, and The Old Mosque, constructed in Edirne in 1404 has nine. The zenith was reached during the period of Süleymaniye the Magnificent and the great architect Sinan built Suleymaniye Mosque in Istanbul, with 13 domes (one main dome, two half domes, and ten small domes) and four minarets, regarded as the most elegant in all the Muslim territories. Sultan Ahmet Mosque in Istanbul, on the other hand, is the only mosque in the world with six minarets.

The Modern Era

In the 18th century, European influence became dominant and Baroque, Rococo and Ampis styles were tried. This is also the period which is called the Tulip Era, because the tulip became a symbol of time and was the major motif in ornamentation, especially in tiles.

After the foundation of the republic, Ottoman fashion gave way to modernism and new buildings with no character started piercing the skyline among the classic masterpieces. Luckily, the enthusiasm to preserve the national heritage developed simultaneously and the restoration of old buildings for use as hotels, restaurants, museums and so on is now quite common.

Suleymaniye Mosque in Istanbul – a grand example of the architectural style of the Ottoman period. (Photo: Turkish Tourist Office)

117

A traditional Turkish wrestling match – a sure sign of a "manly man." (Photo: Turkish Tourist Office)

SPORTS

The Turks love their sport and have a long tradition of competition. Many of the ancient sports have survived into modern times and remain popular, while others have been introduced. Turkish culture tends to embrace anything new and these introduced sports, soccer in particular, have been adopted with typical Turkish fervour.

Wrestling

Wrestling is considered to be the national sport and contests take place throughout the summer in every region. The most prestigious of these contests is the one held in Kırkpınar, where wrestlers coming from all parts of the country compete for the Wrestler of the Year title. It is a very important occasion on the sports calender of Turkey. Tradition requires that the contenders are covered with oil which supposedly makes bodies more slippery and therefore the contest more enjoyable to watch.

Horseback Sports

An Ottoman Turk's horse was his most precious possession, as his mobility depended on it. Even today when people want to emphasise that somebody has managed to finish what you are in the middle of doing, they say, "He who has got the horse, has already reached Üsküdar" (a district in Istanbul) meaning, you are too late, so do not bother. In rural areas horses are still important, together with donkeys, which are owned by the less wealthy but for some reason the Turks have no tradition of horse riding as a form of sport. The only sport they use the horse for is *cirit*, taking its name from the long stick which the riders throw at their rivals to topple them off their mounts.

Football

Today, football (soccer) is the most popular spectator sport and also provides a lot of resources for the provision of sporting facilities through the official football pools. Considering that it was first played in Turkey in 1898 by English merchants in Izmir, the attraction it has created within a century throughout the Turkish population is mind boggling. Incredible sums are paid to foreign clubs for the transfer of prestigious managers and players even by clubs in Anatolia and no one sees any harm in this, even though half of the same amount could bring their local stadium up to Olympic standard.

119

THE CONCEPT OF CLEANLINESS

Hygiene in the home is of utmost importance. A considerable part of the television advertising space is taken up by cleaning products. In a country where dust is extremely intimate and can penetrate into anything in a house even when the windows are closed, perhaps this is not surprising. Nevertheless, stories are recounted about, for instance, one woman who does not let her home-coming husband walk over the threshold before he changes into a complete set of new, clean clothes or about another who washes and dries all the logs before stacking them next to the fire place. These are the extreme cases so they are treated as newsworthy items. What counts as normal is that housewives scrub their wooden floors, boil their white linen in large cauldrons on the cooker before putting it into the washing machine, and never finish washing up before rinsing every item under running water. Very few public launderettes exist in Turkey because people cannot bear to have their washing done in a machine where other people's clothes have been previously washed.

A friend reported his observations of an incident which had taken place in Taksim Square in Istanbul prior to some important local elections. Apparently a major political party was parading in front of masses of people (and votes), with its leader encased in a lavishly decorated coach and a brass band leading the entourage. Suddenly, however, while the band marched on oblivious, the coach stopped. Its driver and henchman got out to clean the sides of the vehicle. With the band by now half a mile up the road, the driver finally returned to his seat and began frantically cleaning his apparently spotless wind-screen while his henchman pointed out the odd speck of dust he had missed in his vigour. Needless to say, the party did not end up winning the election!

The Turks have a minor obsession with cleanliness but the same sensitivity is not always shown by some individuals to what belongs to others. Women shaking the breadcrumbs out of a table cloth from their own balcony on to other people's are not unheard of. Similarly,

I once saw a plastic bag carelessly thrown out of the window of the car in front of us, emptying its contents onto the road before clinging to our windscreen and obscuring our vision.

TURKISH BATHS

During the Ottoman period, when women were confined to the secrecy of their homes, the only public place they could go by themselves was the baths. It was therefore understandable that this was a social location for women in those days and that they wanted to spend the maximum possible time there on each visit, in most cases the whole day, interrupted only by the midday meal which they brought with them in their bags. They talked, exchanged gossip, washed, were cleaned, massaged, perfumed, and additionally, those who had unmarried sons looked for an eligible bride. The baths were open at specific times to males and were popular with men too but they did not have the same social reasons to go there.

Public baths still do good business and one may wonder why. It cannot be for social reasons because the ban on women going out alone does not exist in modern Turkey, nor is there any restriction on them meeting in any other public place (The only places they are not allowed are the men's barbershops and conveniences). Almost all city houses have their own bathrooms now, so the reason cannot be to satisfy a need for personal hygeine either. The answer, in fact, lies in the bloodshot eyes and the dark pink complexions of those leaving the public baths.

The Turkish Massage

A Turkish bath is usually a square or rectangular area with a domed ceiling and many small basins attached along its four walls. Every customer or group of customers takes a basin for individual or group use. The whole place is made of marble which is slippery with the overflowing soap suds, hence the wooden clogs *(nalın)* worn by the bathers. In the middle is the large, communal pool where the water is kept hot by circulation. From the taps of the basins too flows piping hot water. This you mix in the basin with cold water and pour over yourself with a special bowl *(tas)*. On entry the first thing that hits you is the excessive steam. There is not much artificial light in most baths. The glass opening at the top of the dome lets the daylight in.

Clients do not go stark naked there. They cover themselves with a cloth *(pestemal)*. They also bring their own toiletries and the most common type of soap used in a Turkish bath is not the perfumed product found in supermarkets or pharmacies, but a block of green or white, coarse soap. The smell peculiar to this soap may be appreciated only by a few but it is made of olive oil, which is known to be kind to skin and hair alike, and it does not include the dubious chemicals the manufacturers of perfumed, 'quality' soap bars meticulously indicate in small print, if at all.

At the side of the baths there is a raised platform on which the masseurs practise their profession, treating the bodies as if they are kneading dough. Do not make the mistake of saying, *"daha çabuk"* (faster – which you may have learnt to hurry up the taxi driver outside) or you will regret it bitterly. The words you need in this environment are *daha yavas* (lighter) or even *lütfen dur* (please stop). As a different form of massage, he or she may walk on you – literally! The fact that angry mothers say to their mischievious children, "If you keep on doing that, I'll get you under my feet," should not put you off this practice. It is truly rejuvenating and invigorating experience.

Bathers who come in twos or threes can rub one another with a mitt called *kese*, the main attraction in a Turkish bath. The hot steam opens the pores, enabling the bather to rid oneself of all the dirt, dust and dead cells on the skin. In the case of a lone client, an attendant can provide the same service for a small charge. Once the skin is completely clean, the mitt has done its job and this is when you soap yourself for the last time and then leave the premises with bloodshot eyes and a dark pink face.

MEDIA

As it does in most countries, the media has a significant effect on Turkish life. There are few restrictions and both broadcast and print services are fairly reliable sources of information, as well as being ideal ways to improve your language skills.

Television

There are presently more than a dozen national private television channels apart from the five state owned ones in Turkey (TRT1—TRT5). They air a lot of foreign films, mostly dubbed, a lot of home made entertainment shows and a lot of discussion panels. On TRT2, the news and weather are given in English, French and German every day at about 9:30 p.m.

Television is as much a part of the Turkish household as it is in most other developed countries these days. Some argue that this is not always a positive aspect of modern life but for the newcomer the television can provide a valuable source of information, both domestic and international, and has the added advantage of exposing you to the language and customs of your new home.

Radio

Even though most households own a television set, radio has not lost its popularity in Turkey. Until recently, private radio stations were not legal. When the government closed the pirate establishments, it created a big public uproar. Black ribbons were on everybody's collar, and black pieces of cloth on every car antenna. The protest showed no sign of abating and was so earnest that the Government had to pass a law to legalise the stations. Local radio stations are now mushrooming in all parts of the country, at the last count there were more than 5,000 of them in total.

On Turkish radio you will get a good mixture of classical music, jazz, American and European pop and also Turkish music.

Newspapers and Magazines

On the whole, Turkish newspapers are colourful and rich in commentary, with plenty of political, social and economic news of national interest. Apart from one or two of the serious ones, quite a number of them are full of pin-up photographs. The highest circulations belong to *Sabah*, *Hürriyet*, *Milliyet* and *Cumhuriyet*. At the other end of the spectrum, there are some religiously biased newspapers. Among these *Türkiye* has the highest number of subscribers. People buy their paper according to their inclinations, because each paper is known to be a supporter of one political party or another. The only paper in English is the *Daily News* which is published in Ankara but poorly distributed outside the large cities.

Good quality magazines exist and the most popular are *Aktüel*, and *Tempo,* while *Ekonomist* and *Kapital* appeal to the business world. Among those appearing in English, the most attractive is the *Cornucopia Magazine*, which always incorporates interesting articles relating to Turkey and Turkish culture.

Turks love reading newspapers although most cannot afford the pleasure. In rural areas when a bus or a train goes through a station, children run in the same direction, in competition with the moving vehicle. Do not assume that this is a children's game. They are simply reminding you to throw to them the papers and magazines which you have finished reading.

HOLIDAYS

The national holidays in Turkey are based on the international calender and have fixed dates every year. These are:

Jan 1:	New Year's Day
Apr 23:	National Sovereignty and Children's Day
May 19:	Atatürk's Commemoration and Youth and Sports Day
Aug 30:	Victory Day
Oct 29:	National Republic Day

Religious holidays fall on different dates each year because they are regulated by the Islamic calender. The two important religious holidays are called Seker Bayramı (The Feast of Sweets, lasting for three days) and Kurban Bayramı (The Feast of Holy Sacrifice, lasting for four days). Both are periods of merriment when children are given new clothes, the poor are helped and all the family members are visited. Being a Muslim country, Turkey has no Christmas holiday.

Schools break up from the middle of June to early September and also for two weeks in February which are taken as the winter holiday.

— Chapter Seven —

SETTLING DOWN IN TURKEY

TURKISH ATTITUDES TOWARDS FOREIGNERS

For anybody planning to go and settle down in a different country for whatever reason, one of the questions which has to be answered initially is whether or not the inhabitants of this country will be receptive to outsiders. Put your mind at ease if Turkey is your destination. Only a few other places in the world will be as welcoming and accommodating. In these parts, xenophobia is unknown – both as a word and as a feeling.

RENTING A HOUSE

Property agencies exist but they charge both the landlord and the tenant a high commission, which make them extremely unpopular. For this reason a large number of people seek to let or find accommodation through personal enterprise.

Those who need a house or a flat walk at random through the streets to see the sign *"kiralık"* (To Let) in a window, put up there by the landlord, similar to the way the guest houses display the sign "Rooms to let" in their windows. People generally go to property agencies only as a last resort and after many unsuccessful sorties into the chosen areas.

Alternatively, local newspapers have classified advertisements that can be checked every day or friends may know of some empty flats.

BUYING A HOUSE

The purchase of a property by foreigners is a relatively new phenomenon and properties within the military zones or outside the boundaries of the municipalities are still inaccessible for such purposes. Otherwise any foreign national can buy a property, so long as the deed is registered with the Land Registry Office.

To obtain a registration of the title deeds, the buyer must prove to the Land Registry the transfer of the full purchase price into Turkey. Such registration is for a maximum of ten years, renewable, although with the approval of the same office and the Treasury, the initial period can be extended to 15 years. The annual property tax is 0.4% for private buildings and all properties are subject to revaluation every five years for taxation purposes.

Once a property is bought, it may be rented out to others. If the property is subsequently sold, the proceeds from the sale of the property can be transferred out of Turkey, without the imposition of any penalties.

LIVING IN A BLOCK OF FLATS

Individual houses surrounded by their own gardens exist but they are usually well outside the boundaries of the city centre and are ideal only if you have your own transport. The more common type of accommodation in Turkey is the block of flats, or apartments as the Turks prefer to call them.

Life in the flats is very sociable. As soon as you move into one of these blocks, other tenants may come and introduce themselves to you, bring you food, water, and candles (thinking that it will be a day or two before your gas and electricity are connected) and help you with the application for the connection of such amenities. People will ask you all sorts of personal questions to get to know you in a short time and will give you similar information about themselves, as well as some tips about the locality, such as the best local grocery, the whereabouts of the post office and the day of the week when the garbage is collected. In your absence, your neighbours will keep an eye on the visitors as well as strangers who knock on your door and they too will leave their flats in the confidence that you will do the same for them. If you prefer not to mix with them and not to satisfy their curiosity and communal spirit, they will think that you have either something to hide or are too snobbish.

Kapıcı

Within this atmosphere of solidarity, the binding factor is the *kapıcı*. It means, "the one who minds the door" but if you think he is no more than a doorman you will be mistaken. *Kapıcı* is the footman, the handyman, the concierge, the minder, the man-about-the-place, and whatever else you can think of in similar capacities, all in one. In short, he is the *sine qua non* of the block of flats.

The *kapıcı* tradition started with the change that took place in the housing situation after the foundation of the republic. Previously, people had lived in individual houses, one family per house. With the population in the cities growing, the apartment blocks got higher and

The majority of available housing in the cities of Turkey is in large apartment blocks. (Photo: Emlak Kredi)

higher to make room for more and more people and it became essential for someone to take charge of the communal areas of these buildings. But who was going to do this job, and how were the tenants going to subsidise the necessary work force? In those days there was considerable migration from the villages to the cities and the space in the basement next to the main central heating boiler was an ideal place to offer one of these migrant villagers to stay and do the job in return for free accommodation. Once a villager had secured such an arrangement, he got married and brought his bride over. Then he summoned his cousins, neighbours and friends from the same village to come and be *kapıcıs* to other blocks of flats in the same area. In this way, each villager came singly to the city but within a couple of years, expanded his immediate family in the same building, and formed his geographical league in the vicinity.

129

Today, being a *kapıcı* is a 24-hour job. Who cleans the interiors and exteriors of the building as well as doing the gardening, trimming the trees, the shopping (for each flat, twice a day), and the repairing, painting and plumbing? He does. Who turns the central heating on and off daily, as well as regulating it in response to unexpected weather conditions? He does. Who unlocks the main door in the mornings even earlier than the earliest departing tenant, and locks the door after all tenants have returned from their evening engagements? He does. Are you a diabetic who needs a shot of insulin in the middle of the night? Just press the button next to your door for your *kapıcı*. He goes and fetches a nurse for you. Have you left your key indoors by mistake and are you too frightened to climb up to your balcony where the door is unlocked? Do not despair, he will find a ladder to make the operation easy and will even climb it himself to save you the trouble. He takes the letters up to your flat when the postman haphazardly leaves them at the main entrance and the garbage down to the communal waste area when you are too tired to bring it down yourself.

The corner grocery store is an integral part of Turkish life. (Photo: Birlesik Reklamcılar)

He will water your plants and feed your canary while you are on holiday but keep all the street cats and dogs away from the main entrance. He does not have 'itchy feet' either. It is very unusual for a *kapıcı* to change his block – he goes to his grave from where he has started his city life, to be replaced by another *kapıcı* fresh from the village.

OUR GROCERY SHOP

In the residential areas the most frequent shop type is the grocery. There is one or more at every corner, in every street. However, people are not in the habit of buying something from one shop and something else from the other. Every household has a favourite grocery shop which is claimed to be "our grocery shop." This is the shop where people go for their daily bread, newspaper and whatever else they buy regularly or as necessary, unless it has run out of that specific commodity. If it has, then you try somebody else's grocery shop, at the risk of getting pass-the-sell-by-date goods, which are conscientiously saved for occasional customers like you. Grocers know their regulars and are happy to accept payment only once a week, or once a month, depending on how it suits you. It is enough for you to say, "Write it in the book," and you may walk out of the shop with a lorry-load of goods without paying a penny. It is all done in good faith, and both parties know this.

Your grocer will probably be an ex-villager who has been schooled in the cunning atmosphere of a city. The chances are that his apprentice has just come from the village and is being trained by him until he too learns the ropes and opens a grocery shop at another street corner. The first thing an apprentice has to learn is not to let a customer, if it is in his power, walk out of the shop empty handed. He will be told to offer the inquiring customer the nearest thing, if what is asked for is not in stock. For example; "We have no margarine, but the butter is very good," or "We have run out of green olives, but the black olives have just arrived and they are meaty and very tasty."

Some learn quickly, others don't. The apprentice who tells you that he does not have toilet paper but can offer you sand-paper instead still has a long way to go and you can be sure that he will greet you in the same shop for some time to come.

FINDING FURNITURE

Buying second-hand furniture can be problematic. You can start from the small ads section of the newspapers and comb through it daily. There are also some *eskici* (old curiosity) shops or *bit pazarı* (flea markets) where used furniture is on sale but on the whole furniture is either bought from trendy furniture shops downtown, if money is no object, or ordered to be made to the customer's specifications at production sites, which tend to be on the outskirts of a city. If one is not in a hurry, the latter is advisable as the ready made furniture all follows similar fashionable patterns, not necessarily reflecting personal taste or satisfying the needs of comfort, whichever shop you go to, while being on the expensive side at the same time.

There are furnished flats available in those cities where foreigners come to work. The Turks themselves are not in the habit of using other people's furnishings and always go for unfurnished accommodation but the rent of furnished accommodation can be two or three times the price of unfurnished places.

Bringing Furniture from Overseas

Household goods may be brought into Turkey without payment of customs duties by foreigners coming to work in banks, businesses, factories or as official personnel for foreign governments for a minimum of two years. Other foreign residents can similarly avoid customs duties through the temporary import system, as long as one can submit a bank guarantee or similar type of letter ensuring that all customs duties will be paid if these belongings are not taken out of Turkey at the end of the period of residency.

Bedding

Western style duvets are still difficult to find in Turkey because the Turks love their cotton-filled, satin topped quilts, specially made for them by the quilt-maker. As the cotton gets pressed down inside the quilt after regular use, they take the quilt back to the quilt-maker once every two or three years to have the filling fluffed up again. If you have never seen this being done, it is an experience to watch the quilt-maker in action, using his cotton dispenser, while pieces of cotton are flying about in the air, as snow flakes are tossed about by a strong wind in Siberia.

Pillows should be no problem as they come with all possible fillings: cotton, feathers or sponge rubber. In general, the Turks themselves go in for the cotton filled ones, as they are the coolest to sleep on in the long, hot summer. The size might cause some problems for pillow cases brought over from Europe. Those in Turkey are either too long or too small, because the convention is to have the small one put on top of the long pillow, both in their pretty cases frilled with embroidery or lace, matching the quilt cover.

THE BOX ROOM

The exact wording for this place is, in fact, the trunk room. It is a smallish room yet big enough to take a traditional Turkish trunk. It either has no windows, or windows which look out into a stairwell so it is therefore poorly lit. The room and its container have important implications for one's belongings in a country of acute seasonal changes.

Just before the winter, in October, the summer clothes are stored in the trunk so that they will be out of the way for as long as the cold weather lasts. With the coming of May, the summer clothes come out and in go the winter ones. This time, however, more work and celebration are involved, to mark the day as a special one in the family's annual cycle. While older family members are reintroduced to items whose existence they have by now forgotten and try them on for size, the children jump in and out of the trunk, which for a short period offers the attractions of a newly discovered hiding place. In between layers of thick winter garments, naphthalene crystals are sprinkled, with the top layer receiving the most generous handful. Then the trunk is closed tightly and buried in the darkness of the room until the end of the hot season. If this is not done, all woollen clothing will be riddled with hundreds of holes by moths which breed on wool in the hot season.

BATHROOMS AND TOILETS

There are several things that strike a foreigner as different in a Turkish toilet. To start with, the hot and cold water taps usually have a joint outlet. This is to mix the water inside the pipe to the right temperature. The outlet is also long and wide, and distanced from the basin as far as possible.

The reason is that all Turks have what is almost a phobia about not washing their face, or body in still water. It must be running water for them to feel themselves properly cleaned. For this reason, they never

fill the basin with water to wash their face, or the bath tub to soak in. In the tub, you will see either a plastic or copper container (hamam tası) which they use to pour water over themselves while taking a bath, or a shower which simplifies the same exercise. For this reason too, a lot of foreigners are bewildered by the absence of wash basin and bath plugs in Turkey.

If you have to go in your hosts' toilet, they will never expect you to wipe your hands on a towel already there. As soon as you shut yourself in, they will knock on the door to say that a clean towel is attached to the door handle. Indeed, when you open the door again to get it, you will see that you have been treated to the best that they have, one usually stored away in a special drawer with all the other guest towels, laced, embroidered, and fragrant with the scent of the bags of dry lavender beneath which it is kept.

Next to the toilet, you will notice a flip-top waste paper bin, or something similar in appearance. This is for used toilet paper, and is emptied regularly by the hostess. You may at first feel uncomfortable with this method of disposal if you come from a country with a high pressure sewerage system but it avoids the possibility of a blocked toilet and the likely cost of a plumber to come to the house and clear the system.

DOMESTIC HELP

Live-in maids are possible to find but risky. If it is a young girl who comes to take up this position, you have to be very alert to avoid any contact between her and the young males in the vicinity, and this may put a lot of pressure on you. If it is an elderly woman, you will have to deal with her health problems. It is more common to have a home-help who comes to you on a certain weekday or days. You may find this help through the state employment agency, *Is ve Isçi Bulma Kurumu*, but better still through your friends or your *kapıcı*.

Home-help is supposed to cover much more than it does in most other countries. To start with, it is a full day's work, from 9 to 5. Also, it involves the cleaning, scrubbing, washing or polishing of every-thing – the floors, the furniture, the balconies, the doors and the windows. In some households, it even involves doing the dishes, the ironing and polishing the silver. The pay ranges from $US10 to $US20 per day, depending on the size of the flat as well as the district.

BRINGING A CAR TO TURKEY

If you are in Turkey as a working foreigner and you want to acquire a car, the first thing you must do is look at its number plate. A white number plate on a car means all the Turkish duties have been paid. You can buy a new car from a dealer duty free, which will make it about 30% cheaper but in this case you have to apply for a blue number plate to show that the car belongs to a foreigner.

Alternatively you can bring your foreign plate car, or buy one from a departing foreigner but unless you apply for a blue plate for it, the car has to be taken out of Turkey every three months. Blue plate cars can be bought from other foreigners as well and the best place to find these is in the *Yabancıdan Yabancıya* (Foreigner to Foreigner) column in the daily paper. Road tax is collected twice a year and is compulsory for everybody.

Driving Licence

Every visitor driving in Turkey must hold an international licence, issued in his or her country of origin. This can be used during stays of up to one year after which time it is necessary to obtain a Turkish licence. The documents for this can be obtained from the applicant's embassy or consulate in Turkey. Additionally one is supposed to have the car licence (documents with all the details relating to the car), international green card (insurance) and transit book (*carnet de passage*, for those who want to proceed to the Middle East). Traffic circulates on the right and the Turkish Highway Code is similar to those of European countries. There is a 50 k.p.h. speed limit in urban centres and a 90 k.p.h. limit outside the city boundaries.

Petrol Stations and Garages

There are numerous repair garages in towns and they are usually grouped along special streets. They are also well distributed, like the petrol stations, over all roads and the main highways. Outside big cities, one cannot normally pay by credit card. Unleaded petrol is available at most stations, although prices are variable.

There is not an organisation like the Automobile Association, so if you have a breakdown in the middle of nowhere, you have to wait for another motorist to give you a lift to the nearest garage or call a towing company to come to your aid.

EDUCATION FOR FOREIGN CHILDREN

There are schools in Turkey established by foreign organisations but they all operate under the jurisdiction of the Turkish Ministry of Education. Schools such as the English High School, the French Dame de Sion, St. Benoit, and St. Joseph, the Italian High School and the American Colleges in Istanbul, Izmir and Tarsus, have some lessons in the language of origin but also provide lessons in Turkish.

Those parents who wish their children to have education only in their mother tongue should contact their embassies in Ankara to see if there is a school within the embassy grounds. The British, American and French embassies have such facilities for the children of their diplomatic staff but accept outsiders too.

SERVICES AND UTILITIES

Post Office

Post offices in Turkey are the outlets of PTT (Turkish Post, Telephone and Telegraph Organisation) and are recognisable by their bright yellow signs. Some Europeans who are accustomed to buying sweets, chocolates, toys, or pretty wrapping paper in a post office in their own country will be surprised that the Turkish equivalent is concerned only with matters relating to the post, telephone, telegraph and fax.

That means you can buy a stamp, a *jeton* (a token to use the telephone) or a telephone card, post a letter, make a call, send a telegram, dispatch or receive a fax, apply for a telephone line or pay your phone bill, but this is all you can do in a post office.

Foreigners living in Turkey need to beware of goods sent to them by surface rather than airmail. On the European side of Istanbul all such parcels are dispatched to a central depot (at Topkapı) from where the process of retrieving them is tortuous. After hours of waiting and signing, you sometimes walk away clutching your parcel and wishing that the sender had not been so kind in the first place.

Public Telephones

Public telephones operate on a system of *jetons* or plastic cards, sold at PTT offices. Small *jetons* are used for local calls, and middle sized ones for intercity calls, while the largest are for international calls.

When making intercity calls, one has to dial the city code, then the numbers. For an international call, it is necessary to dial 0 twice to get an international line and then the country and the area codes followed by the number.

Before 1986, to have a telephone line connected to your house could have been a long process, requiring endless patience, unless you knew someone important in high places. In some cases it was as long as a year or two between the application and connection dates, as the demand was greater than PTT's existing resources. This has fortunately changed with the modernisation of the telephone system in the second half of the 1980s. Now people do not have to wait for months on end to be connected, it takes only a couple of weeks. For this service, one contacts the local PTT.

Water and Electricity

These two amenities are run by the municipalities, which operate on an independent but very tight budget although they do receive some subsidy from the government.

In Turkey do as the Turks do – keep candles or gas lamps and buckets of water in reserve because there will certainly be cuts and such a reserve will come in handy. Cuts may be regular, that is, on certain days and at certain times, which is a nuisance but as long as you are well stocked, you can still live through them. On the other hand, there may also be unexpected, surprise cuts, at a time when you are least prepared for them – when entertaining important guests, or in the middle of taking a bath, for example.

Foreigners who are not accustomed to living in such surprise conditions should be extremely careful not to leave their accommo-

Power cuts are still quite common in Turkey but schemes like the Hasan Ugurlu Hydro-electric Project have made electricity supplies a little more reliable in recent years. (Photo: Turkish Tourist Office)

139

dation without checking first that they have turned off all the water taps. A tap that is left on is as harmless as one that is turned off when there is no water but once the water returns the whole flat, as well as the flat of the downstairs neighbour, is in danger of being flooded if there is no one around to turn it off.

Some small hotels and guesthouses are also known to apply their own water cuts during certain hours of the day to reduce water bills, and need to be told off seriously if they should practise this. Putting your head out of the window and shouting downstairs, "Water!" each time you wish to take a shower neither solves the problem permanently nor lifts one's holiday spirits.

Gas

Almost all cooking appliances in Turkey work on gas because it is cheaper than electricity, but the form of gas for domestic use is not uniform. Turkey does not have enough natural gas supplies to satisfy its needs and mainly imports it from some of the neighbouring countries.

Natural gas connections have already been made for most areas in Ankara and some areas in Istanbul where both the stoves and central heating systems benefit from the provision but in Turkey the majority of people still buy a gas cylinder to work their stove. There are several makes on sale in the market and the companies that offer better services can be recommended by the *kapıcı*.

It may be helpful to know at this stage that having a stove that works on a gas cylinder is not as troublesome as it sounds. All you have to do when you run out of gas is to ring your supplier and he will immediately send you a new container and relieve you of the old one at the same time. That is, as long as this happens during office hours. Alternatively, you can hail a passing gas canister vendor in the street. They come by regularly every day. Careful housewives keep a close eye on their gas stock and more careful ones keep a spare supply in the cupboard.

MEDICAL CARE

There are some foreign hospitals scattered all over Turkey. In Ankara the American Hospital *(Balgat Amerikan Tesisleri)*; in Istanbul the French Hospital *(Sisli)*, the Italian Hospital *(Tophane)*, the German Hospital *(Taksim)*, International Hospital *(Yesilköy)*, the English Admiral Bristol Hospital *(Nisantası)* and the Jewish Hospital *(Ayvansaray)*; in Izmir another Jewish Hospital *(Inönü Caddesi);* and in Gaziantep the second American Hospital.

Apart from these there are very good, private hospitals in Ankara, Istanbul and Izmir and advice can be sought regarding these at the local pharmacies.

Pharmacies

The pharmacies are open from 9:00 a.m. to 7:00 p.m. but a 24-hour service is provided by them in rotation. To find out which pharmacies are open after seven o'clock in your area, consult the *nöbetçi ezcaneler* (pharmacies on duty) section of your local newspaper.

At the pharmacy you can get first-aid, as well as medical advice. Additionally, you can have your injections given to you there. If you are too ill to go out, the pharmacy can arrange for the local nurse to come to your house to give you an injection. State hospitals are notorious for their waiting lists and private ones for their heavy charges so a large number of people go to pharmacies first. As many drugs are sold over the counter without a doctor's prescription, only persistent ailments cause patients to resort to the hospitals.

BARBERS AND HAIRDRESSING SALONS

In Turkey it is unusual to find unisex hair salons. It is either a barber's shop for men, or a hairdresser's shop for women, and among the skilled workers, these professionals deserve a mention because of the complete service they provide.

In a barber's shop, the beard or moustache is shaved or trimmed, the hair is cut, shampooed and dried, the scalp is massaged, the hair

141

in or on the nose and ears is removed, the neck is powdered and brushed, until eventually one emerges from the bundle of towels and layers of foam somehow a cleaner, shinier, leaner, in short, a different person. And this is all done amidst a lively conversation.

It cannot be a coincidence that all barbers are extremely talkative by nature. I sometimes think that perhaps when the apprentices are being trained by the master craftsmen, they are taught how to talk and thus distract the customer's attention from the straight razor *(ustura)* they are using to perform their art. Cutting the hair with scissors is what your wife does at home. A professional barber never demeans himself with such inartistic tools. While the comments on the latest football results make your blood boil, the *ustura* crops a lock from the right. When you are into discussing the love life of a famous film star the *ustura* gets a patch from the middle. The left side has its share during references to the latest inflation figures. The barber stops his talk all of a sudden and shakes the uppermost towel and this is when you finally notice the *ustura* and see yourself in the mirror for the first time since you sat in front of it.

A hairdresser is equally chatty but on more feminine topics. His role is to entertain rather than distract. All the local gossip accompanies the complete treatment of dyeing, highlighting, cutting, trimming, blow-drying, and much more. With your limbs stretched in all directions like a tourist on a sunny beach, you have one girl to deal with your manicure, another with your pedicure, and a third one with the unwanted hair on your legs. A young boy holds the hair-dryer to the parts of your hair indicated periodically by the chin of the artist, and an even younger boy positions the mirror to show you the miracles his master has performed behind your back.

Throughout the treatment, you feel like an empress, surrounded by various servants, all at your service. You come to your senses and realise what a large and unnecessary workforce is employed in a hairdresser's shop when it is time to give tips, slipped discreetly into the pockets of all attendants, in various amounts depending on status, while the lion's share goes into that of the master craftsman.

Chapter Eight

DOING BUSINESS IN TURKEY

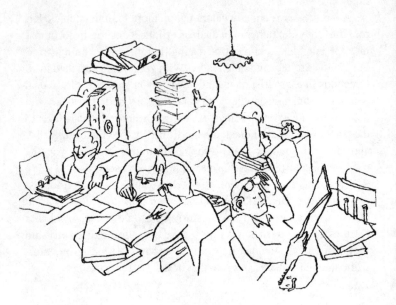

AN ENTRY VISA

For some nationalities, an entry visa is required for visits not exceeding three months and you can find out whether or not this applies to your own nationality by contacting the Turkish embassy in your country. An entry visa is usually obtained at the port of entry by paying a small amount of money (for instance, it is £10 sterling for British tourists).

VISAS TO RESIDE OR WORK IN TURKEY

If you wish to reside in Turkey longer than the normal three month period allowed to tourists, or to set up a business, you will need a residence visa. This type of visa can be obtained through a Turkish Consulate General in any country. People who are planning to stay in Turkey for business reasons must additionally have a work visa issued by the appropriate Turkish Consulate General before arriving in Turkey. If the stay is related to research, cave exploration or mountain climbing, visa applications are made to the Turkish Embassy.

On arrival in the country, the next step is to register with the local police headquarters within a month of arrival and obtain a residence permit. The maximum duration of a residence permit is two years. Residence permits are sometimes retained by the police when the visitor leaves Turkey but they will be returned upon re-entry to the country.

Transit visas are not required for passengers continuing their journey to a third country.

FINDING A JOB IN TURKEY

Finding a job in Turkey is not the easiest thing for foreign nationals because one has to find a job and apply for a work visa before arriving in the country and job advertisements seldom appear in newspapers or journals of foreign origin. A possible source of help is the Turkish employment agency, the address of which is:

Is ve Isçi Bulma Kurumu,
Cemal Gürsel Caddesi 8/A
Sıhhıye
Ankara.

Although this agency primarily serves the needs of the Turks themselves, there may be occasional jobs on offer for foreigners.

The situation for teachers of English, however, is more encouraging as there is a constant demand for these professionals in large cities, and a number of teaching institutions regularly place advertisements in the British and American newspapers and periodicals.

It is important to secure an employment contract, which must subsequently be approved by the Turkish Ministry of Education, Ministry of Tourism or State Planning Organisation, depending on the nature of the work. This contract will be required by the consulate granting the work visa. Even after you pass this stage, if you decide to change your job while you are in Turkey, make sure that you do not start your new job before signing a new contract. Some business enterprises are in the habit of not offering contracts to evade tax responsibilities, and unless you sign a contract you are running the risk of being fired with immediate dismissal and no compensation.

BUSINESS IN TURKEY

There was a big influx of foreign capital into Turkey when the government eased regulations governing this in 1980. The amount of foreign capital invested in the country from 1954 to 1980 was US$228 million, but in 1991 alone, permission for US$251 million to enter Turkey was granted. Apart from banking, the most popular areas for investment are tourism, the automotive industry, military aircraft, electronics, food and agriculture, construction and mining.

Foreign companies, resident or nonresident, doing business in Turkey may qualify for a number of allowances, deductions or exemptions under corporate income tax law. The State Planning Organisation issues a publication in English listing all possible incentives and interested individuals or firms may apply for a copy.

Companies are formed in the form of Corporations (A.S.), Limited Partnerships (Ltd.) or Private Limited Companies (TLS), although the last are rare. Tax laws and owner liabilities make the A.S. and Ltd. companies more advantageous. A corporation with more than a hundred shareholders is registered on the Stock Exchange.

Foreign nationals may establish companies without the necessity of there being a Turkish national in the company. They may bring an unlimited amount of foreign currency into Turkey for investment purposes. They can open bank accounts in foreign currency, and can freely transfer the profits out of the country subject to the payment of local taxes. They can apply for bank credits as long as they provide documents and goods to be used against these credits. Once a business has been established in Turkey, all Turkish laws and regulations which normally apply to Turkish citizens will automatically apply to them too.

DOING BUSINESS WITH THE TURKS

Personal relationships are the key to success for a business enterprise in Turkey, where who you know is sometimes more important than what you know. In a business conversation, never be in a hurry to get to the point. Start with pleasantries and friendly exchanges before you come to the crunch.

In general, most Turks find it difficult to be punctual for business meetings as they are too relaxed to keep to a rigid timetable. If the meeting is held outside their place of business, they are often delayed by the traffic, which, of course, is beyond their control. Is the same tolerated in a foreigner who has a meeting with a Turkish company? The answer is yes, as long as one can find a good excuse for it, but the larger a company is, the more experienced they are in detecting phoney excuses, so to be on the safe side, be punctual.

Business Opportunities

In the days of the Ottoman Empire, business was an area left to the minorities. The Turks got interested in doing business themselves only after the republic had been established. Despite this late start they have taken large strides. They still have things to learn but even so it is interesting to know that, for instance, the second largest tomato exporting company in Europe today is based in Turkey (TAT A.S.).

During the years 1920–1945 Turkey simply tried to make ends meet, just as most of Europe did at the time. From the 1950s onwards, it dawned on the Turks that a closed economy would take the country nowhere, so people became interested in earning their living abroad. Large numbers went to Germany to work. In the 1970s, Arabic speaking countries, especially Libya and Saudi Arabia, with their huge construction projects became points of attraction. After a lull, it is now Russia, the Balkans and the central Asian republics that are providing cash opportunities for a considerable number of Turkish companies.

The Turks have a knack of knowing where the money is. You can see the street vendors congregating at all major crossroads, stadium, mosque and school entrances, public transport stops, all places where there will be crowds. I was not surprised to hear that a number of Turks in Germany made themselves quite rich on the night the Berlin Wall was pulled down. Apparently they sold shish-kebabs all night in push-trolleys which they had bought the day before for the occasion.

MARKETING

Most liberal economy marketing tactics are in operation in Turkey. The incentives given to the consumer usually take the form of a free bonus. A washing powder company advertises that if you take two empty boxes to the shops, you will receive two packets of margarine. A margarine company says that by sending in five wrappers from their product, you will receive a free bottle of shampoo. A shampoo company offers you the chance of going to Paris if you collect a certain number of their bottles.

In this competition, however, nothing is as fierce as the war among the newspapers. Three major papers have been competing for several years now in offering bigger and better giveaways, starting with modest books, then going into complete sets of encyclopedia. Currently they are into tableware and bedding. As soon as one gives away a cutlery set for 30 or so newspaper coupons, the others offer sets of pots and pans, crystal ware, stainless steel kitchen knives, bed linen and table cloths, to name but a few of the more recent incentives.

In this modern Turkish office new marketing ideas are being tested before being unleashed on the consumer. The marketing sometimes overshadows the product in Turkey as advertisers seek out new ways to sell their product. (Photo: BBDO Turkey)

Recently, one of these papers advertised that it would give all its readers an electronic translator with the capacity to cover five different languages and a market price of nearly $200. In a country where the newspaper readership is not very high and the price of a newspaper is so low, none of the newspapers are expecting to make a profit from giving so much to and receiving so little from the readership. Indeed, what they have fixed their eyes on is not the readers' pockets but a larger slice of the advertising cake, which runs into billions of dollars every year. And as it is the reader who benefits from all this, the government is letting the battle of the giants carry on.

However, first things first and before you convince the consumer to buy your product, you need to alert him or her to your existence. Along the quays of the yacht harbour in Marmaris, there is a long line of street vendors to attract the tourists. A section of this queue of vendors is occupied by people with a very strange trade – they carve your name on a grain of rice under a microscope and place it in a little glass horn full of water (to magnify the object and its script) which you can then wear as a pendant. In front of each vendor there is a sign advertising this service. On one of these posters I saw an English sentence: "Your name carve on a piece of rice." I suddenly felt the urge to correct the mistake and stopped. "There is a mistake here," I said, "you should have written 'Your name *carved* on a grain of rice.'" The young man behind the counter smiled. "I know that," he said gaily. Then, seeing the surprise on my face, he gave an explanation. "If I had used the correct sentence, no one would have stopped, but this way I am catching the attention of the tourists more than my rivals here."

Similarly, I heard from the managing director of a famous fruit juice company that on half of their products for the home market, they put the labels on the cans upside down. Apparently, due to this gimmick, on a shelf full of similar cans selling the same product, his products catch the eye of the consumer first and give his company the brand name recognition they seek.

Whatever the advertising method, you should be very careful about what you are buying and whether or not the vendor has the right to sell it. The case which hit the headlines in the 1960s still brings smiles to the faces of those old enough to remember it. A naive villager on his first visit to Istanbul was admiring the Galata Tower – a famous and historic tower, which is to this city what the Eiffel Tower is to Paris or Big Ben to London. The visitor could not believe his luck when he was approached by the 'owner' of the tower who offered to sell it to him for all the money he had in his pocket at the time (which as it happened was a considerable sum). It was only when the proud new owner of the tower went to the registration office to collect his property deed and make his purchase official that he realised he had been tricked.

INCOME TAX

Diplomats and officials working for agencies of foreign countries are exempted from income tax. All other foreigners whose stay in Turkey exceeds six months, must pay the tax, except for journalists and scholars whose presence in Turkey is for a specific, temporary job.

Income tax rates may vary depending on the amount of income earned. For people who are in the low income bracket the rate is 25% but it can go up to 50% for the highest earners. Preferential rates are applied to the wages of people whose work is in the first and second priority areas for development.

ATTIRE AND ATTITUDE IN THE OFFICE

People put on their 'respectable' clothes to go to work. A suit and tie is a must for men, and the latter is not loosened even on the hottest day. Women are also supposed to present a respectable front but the rules of attire are less strict for working women. The only expectation is that women dress neatly and decently but what this means is not always clearly defined. What it meant in the parliament in 1995 was made clear by one of the MPs when he asked a female television journalist to leave the chamber because she was not wearing tights. This was despite the fact that it was summer and the poor woman had a longish

dress to cover most of her bare legs anyway. Foreigners working in Turkey are often dismayed by demands that they should dress smartly at all times during working hours – far more so than, say, in English workplaces; dress-sense, or lack of it, is considered a good indication of your seriousness towards your job.

There is a strict, almost regimental ordering of ranks in the office. The juniors are supposed to demonstrate their respect for their seniors in particular ways. They must wear their jackets buttoned up in their seniors' presence, they must open the doors for them and stand up when they walk in. As the hierarchy is manifold, those at the top end are the most relaxed while those at the bottom live on their dreams of promotion.

Hademe

In every office but especially in those belonging to the civil service, there is a *hademe,* who is basically an errand boy – although *hademes* are usually in their forties or older. They do the odd jobs like bringing in glasses of tea (this is the drink most often consumed in an office), taking documents from one office to another for signature, informing the junior workers of their visitors, cleaning and other odd jobs. Such activities do not keep the *hademe* occupied from nine to five, so it is more customary to see him sitting aimlessly on a wooden chair in the corridor until a worker puts his head out of the office door and calls him.

As competition in every sector is getting harder and people are tying to find ways to cut down on their expenses, there is a general consensus growing that a company does not need so many of its *hademes* (in some work places there is one on every floor), or that it can even do without them altogether. The luxury of disposing of the *hademes*, however, belongs only to the private sector. The state sector, with the present high unemployment figures at hand, will have to live with the system until new posts are created to employ this work force in a more productive way.

Business or Social Cards?

Turkish people are not in the habit of exchanging business cards as soon as they meet as is the custom in many cultures. They prefer to talk and test the water before they decide whether or not to give their cards. They will not waste them in encounters with no future prospects. If you walk out of the conversation with a card in your hand, you can be sure that you will hear from the card owner sometime in the future.

Business cards have other functions too. They may be left on your door to indicate the caller's identity. They may be stapled to cards for Christmas or Muslim festivities or they may be attached to a bunch of flowers or other gift items. As most signatures in Turkey are artistic scribbles, containing straight or curved lines, circles, dots and some geometric forms, business cards help the recipient to identify the sender.

MONEY MATTERS

The Turkish lira is in constant depreciation. This trend has continued for such a long time and the zeros on the price tags have formed such a long train that the possibility of dropping several noughts, to make life easy for everybody, is now being seriously considered. Because of this creeping trend, people prefer doing business, especially when renting houses and offices, in American dollars.

The Turks hate asking for money unless in a totally commercial context. Even then you may have to slide the money into a recipient's side pocket, when for instance tipping a barber or a hotel bellboy, while the recipient pretends not to notice.

In repaying a debt, never give the money openly and never at the beginning of an encounter. Always place the bank-notes in an envelope and pass it over at the last minute, as if it is something you have remembered accidentally. The recipient will not look at it twice and will put it out of sight straightaway as if you have handed over something useful but quite unmentionable.

Banks

Foreign banks have operated in Turkey since the 19th century. The Franco-British Ottoman Bank *(Osmanlı Bankası)* was founded in 1863. The Dutch Hollandse Bank-Unie opened in 1921 and the Banco di Roma, belonging to the Italians, also dates back to the Ottoman times.

By the end of 1990 there were a large number of banks operating in Turkey: The Central Bank *(Merkez Bankası)*, 56 commercial banks, including 33 national banks, 16 foreign banks with branches in Turkey and 7 incorporated banks. However, according to their assets, the top five banks in Turkey are:

- TC Ziraat Bankası
- Türkiye Is Bankası
- Türk Emlak Bankası
- Akbank
- Yapı ve Kredi Bankası

Foreigners may keep their money in the form of foreign currency by opening a foreign exchange deposit account in a bank that is authorised to change foreign currency and all five listed above fall into this category.

Foreign Exchange

It is possible to change any foreign currency into Turkish lira in most banks and even at the 'currency kiosks' temporarily set up at tourist resorts. Changing Turkish lira back into foreign currency, is similarly easy. You simply have to go to a local exchange shop and they will do it for you.

The current rate of exchange is monitored by the Central Bank, although the percentage put on the base by the individual banks differs to some extent. For this reason, it is best to check the offers by various banks before having the transaction done. You are advised not to have

The banking industry in Turkey is generally modern and efficient. (Photo: Yapı Kredi)

all your money changed at once. Even within a period of two weeks, you may get a better rate for your currency.

In your daily life in Turkey, you will be surprised to see how tattered some of the bank notes are. You can have these changed at any bank for new, crisp ones, so it is not a disaster if a shop keeper gives you a worn out, partly torn bank note. The only thing you need to be careful about is that the note is complete, and is not missing a part, however tiny it may be. Incomplete bank notes are rejected both by individuals and by banks, except for Merkez Bankası (Central Bank of Turkey).

Credit Cards

It is possible to use the main credit cards, i.e. Visa, American Express, Mastercard and Diners Club, in large department stores, hotels and restaurants in the big cities and where tourists are found in large numbers. You can even use these cards to draw Turkish lira from the cash-points, although this service is available only at a small number of banks. The lowest amount that can be drawn in this way from a bank in 1996 is TL250,000.

RED TAPE

"A lot of action in a short time" is the motto in the private sector, where red tape is at its minimum. If the normal working day is not long enough to finish what is in the work tray, people work overtime with no claims for the extra payment.

Fulfilling the promise of this motto requires speed and in some cases things move so quickly that it may become baffling for an outsider. In contrast, a Turkish friend who was buying a house in England expressed his frustration after weeks of paperwork between the solicitors (his and the seller's) and said, "This is like torture. I miss Turkey where you go and see a house, agree on the price with the seller, and on the same day you shake hands with him, which means the transaction is complete."

Go Today, Come Back Tomorrow

The speed and practicality which prevails in the private sector is nonexistent in the state one. There the work pace is very slow. So slow that in case you have to get a residence permit endorsed, or wait in queues to see a doctor, or receive a state pension, you may have to, as people say in ridicule of the system, "go today and come back tomorrow."

Some of this is due to the relaxed attitude of the civil servants. Most of them are placed in the job with someone important backing them so they are secure, but it is also because the bureaucracy and impracticality are engrained in the system. I had to pay my electricity bill and visited the town hall one afternoon. As I was there to pay rather than to receive, I thought it would take only a couple of minutes. How mistaken I was! It was almost an hour before I could leave the building. First I had to wait for Miss X on the second floor, then I was sent downstairs to see Mr Y, who signed my bill after checking it against his figures and asked me to go up to Miss X again. Miss X, however, had in the meantime become involved with another applicant. When she was finally free to see me again, she asked me to go one floor up to buy an official stamp for the document. On the third floor the man selling stamps was busy on the phone so I had to wait for the conversation to finish. Then I brought the document down to Miss X who told me to go to the cashier on the first floor. When I had completed the whole thing, I was out of breath from running up and down stairs so many times. If you have to go to a civil service office for any reason, just allow yourself plenty of time and do it when your energy is not at its lowest ebb.

TECHNOLOGY

Following the World Wars, Turkey's economy was not in a position to keep pace with technological advances and their import was delayed for a very long time. When television started in 1968 with the test programmes two hours a day, people used to queue up outside the shop windows, watching the screen in amazement and admiration.

Today it is a different story. Technological novelties are immediately brought into Turkey as people are keen to use them. One craze follows another. There were the days when everybody installed musical bells on their doors and musical waiting devices on their telephones. We are now in the age of home computers, faxes, and mobile phones. The whole world is in the sitting room of every household, whether it is in a metropolitan suburb or a remote Anatolian village, thanks to satellite dishes and cables.

The hunger for everything new is insatiable. When years ago the director of a major white goods company producing cooking appliances, fridges, washing machines and the like told me that he was planning to introduce microwave ovens into the Turkish market, I had my doubts about the initiative. I thought an appliance which is good where frozen food is consumed a lot would not be similarly popular in Turkey, where people love to cook using fresh ingredients. I was wrong. Today, microwave ovens are to be found in the kitchens of all those who can afford them. They cook, they bake, they even make their Turkish coffee in them.

Of course, disappointment is experienced from time to time. A television programme reported in 1995 that an Istanbul district municipality had imported from Italy ultramodern toilet cabins and set them up at various points in their area. Only after the cabins had been installed and the first customer went into one to test it did people realise that one needed Italian money to open the doors again. So the same customer was confined in this tight situation until an Italian tourist was found in the vicinity and the right coin was extracted from him.

Problems also arise when something goes wrong with such technological wonders. It is one thing to import the technology, it is another to provide maintenance and repair services and the latter seem more difficult to obtain. On the subject of technological breakdown, I shall never forget the sign next to a lift in a block of flats. It said: "This lift is out of order. The nearest functioning lift is in the building across the road."

WORKING HOURS

The hours of business in Turkey vary according to the activity involved. Here is a list of the trading hours of some of the more important offices and shops. The times are given using the 24-hour clock system, which is used to tell the time in Turkey:

Banks:	8.30 – 12.00/13.30 – 18.00
Business offices:	8.30 – 17.00 or 9.00 – 18.00
Museums:	8.30 – 12.30/13.30 – 17.00
Post offices:	8.30 – 12.30/13.30 – 17.30
Main P.O.	Open 24-hours daily
Shops:	9.00 – 19.00 (although small shops in residential districts or tourist areas may close at a later time)
Travel agencies:	8.30 – 18.00 (Monday to Friday) 9.00 – 13.00 (Saturday)

DATES AND NUMBERS

Dates are written in a particular sequence: the date first, then the month, then the actual day, followed by the year: 10 Agustos Persembe, 1995 (10 August Thursday, 1995).

Numbers are written with a dot denoting thousands and a comma instead of the decimal point: 1.000.000,00 is one million.

The percentage has a different sequence from the English version. In Turkish it is %90 instead of 90%.

INTERNATIONAL TIME

Turkey is two hours ahead of Greenwich Mean Time so when it is noon in London, it is 14.00 (2:00 p.m.) in Istanbul. In summer (end of March to the end of September) clocks are moved one hour forward but as the same is done in England, the difference remains constant.

CULTURAL QUIZ

Now that you have some insight into the Turkish way of life you may like to try this quiz to test your knowledge. There are very few problems that can't be overcome by taking the basic elements of Turkish culture into account. The long history of cultural integration, the geographical location and the hospitality of the Turks make getting to know Turkey one of the most rewarding experiences in travel.

SITUATION ONE

You have just moved into a new flat. Your next door neighbour appears at your door with her three young children beside her and a tray of shish-kebabs in her hands. It is nice to be thought of in this way but you are a vegetarian. What is more, you do not fancy jumping into a sudden friendship with such a large family. What will you do?

A. Take the meal as if it was a great favour and return the empty tray to your neighbour the next day, having disposed of its contents in the way you think fit.

B. Thank her for her kindness but tell her you cannot accept the offer as you are a vegetarian.

C. Tell her that you are well stocked with food so she should give the meal to someone else who would appreciate it more.

Comments

New tenants being treated to cooked food by their neighbours on their arrival is an old custom in Turkey. The idea behind it is that on such a day, you are too occupied with other things so you have neither the time nor the resources to prepare a meal for yourself and your family.

If you go for option **B** and refuse the food on the grounds that you are a vegetarian, your neighbour will probably take the kebabs back but then will go to the trouble of preparing you a vegetable dish instead.

Refusing the meal on the pretext that you do not need it and suggesting that it should be given to someone else is an insult and therefore should be avoided completely.

The most diplomatic course to take, under the circumstances, is option **A** but note that you should still not return the tray empty. Put into it some sweets, or chocolates, or biscuits, or whatever else you may have, before giving it back.

SITUATION TWO

You realise that the young girl who stays with you as a home-help is romantically involved with the brother of the *kapıcı*. Although her attitude to her work is not affected you feel that the relationship may cause complications within the apartment block you are living in if the matter becomes the subject of local gossip. What will you do?

- **A.** Tell her that you are totally against this relationship and that she will be sent back to her parents unless she behaves herself.
- **B.** Rather than giving her a second chance, send her back to her parents immediately, informing them of the reasons.
- **C.** Turn a blind eye to the fact, thinking that the girl is over 18 and what she does in her spare time is none of your business?

Comments

The girl has probably been brought to your house in the first place by her parents who assumed that you would be acting as her 'second parents' and most parents are not tolerant to their daughters having romantic attachments, irrespective of the age.

Therefore option **C** is definitely not what you should do, although you might argue that this is the most common course to take in your own country.

Under the circumstances, you should choose between immediate dismissal or warning before dismissal depending on how far the relationship has developed.

In this way, you will be protecting yourself from any future accusations by the real parents, should the affair become common knowledge to everybody.

SITUATION THREE

Each time you go and buy something from your grocer he says Turkish goods are the best and the cheapest in the world and insists that every item that you buy from his shop is of far better quality than it could possibly be in your country. In the first couple of instances, you took it light-heartedly but as he repeats the same estimation parrot-like at each encounter, and obviously takes pleasure in it, it is now getting on your nerves. What will you do?

A. Tell him to shut up and prepare the goods as you have no time and patience for such pointless comparisons.

B. Change your grocery shop and find a quieter grocer in the vicinity, even if it means walking further down the road each way.

C. Enjoy the game by reversing the roles and taking the words from his mouth, saying that you would have paid a lot more for your purchase had it been in your country – although it is not true.

Comments

National pride is in the blood of every Turk and you will not be avoiding it by simply changing locations. Nor will it help to argue with them on such points.

Although Turkish people are not without a sense of humour, you may be entering dangerous territory if you joke about national or cultural issues too blatantly, so sarcasm or poking fun at Turkish products is not a healthy option.

The best advice here is to learn how to respect their sensitivity to national matters and while doing so you may even find ways to enjoy yourself.

Taking all these into account, you will see that option **C** is the best choice in the list.

SITUATION FOUR

You are visiting an ancient site when all of a sudden a street vendor approaches and puts one of his ancient looking busts in your hand. *"Bir milyon"* he says. You do not need an interpreter to understand that he is trying to sell the bust to you for the once in a lifetime price of one million lira. However, you are not terribly interested in buying the artifact. What will you do?

A. Put the bust on the ground and walk away.

B. Say, *"Yarım milyon"* (half a million) thinking that you will get rid of him by halving his price.

C. Say no in the most decisive way and try to give the bust back to him.

Comments

You may try to give the bust back to him but what guarantees that he will take it back immediately? He will most probably dodge your attempts. If this is how the case develops, you may find it easier to pay him rather than making him repossess the item, which means option **C** is not the ideal solution.

If you try to discourage him by halving his price as in option **B**, you will give the impression that you are a potential buyer who is bargaining. As a result, the man may agree with the price you have given him and wait for his payment.

In a situation like this, the most important thing to remember is that ancient sites are dangerous locations where the goods on sale may be real antiques, the purchasing of which is a punishable act.

To be on the safe side, the best way to go is to put the article on the ground and walk away as option **A** suggests, although it is the least polite way of dealing with the situation.

SITUATION FIVE

The taxi you board takes off as soon as you show the driver a piece of paper on which the address you wish to go is written. However, after a while you realise that the man at the wheel has no idea where he is going because he is stopping a passer-by every now and then to ask for directions. What should you do?

A. Stop the car immediately, pay the driver and look for another one.

B. Let the man find his way somehow but pay him less than the amount on the taxi meter once you finally arrive at your destination.

C. Ask the man to take you to the nearest police station instead so that you can make your complaint there.

Comments

Of course none of these is the ideal solution to the problem. If you choose option **A** you will reward the driver for his unprofessional attitude.

If you ask him to take you to the nearest police station (of course he may refuse but let us assume for the sake of argument that he obliges) you will be punishing him, but on the other hand you will be punished too because you will spend several hours at the station.

You may opt for the last choice of allowing the driver to find the address eventually after the umpteenth attempt to get directions, but be prepared for an argument when you offer him less than the amount showing on his meter at the end of the journey (option **B**).

All these can be avoided if you make sure before getting in the taxi that its driver knows where he is taking you.

SITUATION SIX

You are entertaining an important guest for dinner and all of a sudden the power gets cut off. You look out of your window and see that the man who lives across the road is in his sitting room, sipping tea and happily watching the big football match on television. What will you do?

- **A.** Call your *kapıcı* to come to your apartment and fix your power supply box.
- **B.** Locate the power supply box, find your toolbox and fix it yourself, probably by candlelight.
- **C.** Assume that it is a local cut and wait for the return of the power.

Comments

Electricity and water are not always the most reliable commodities in Turkey and power failures and loss of water supply are things that people learn to live with.

Many people keep a backup supply of water in bottles or jugs and it would be rare to find a home without a supply of candles.

Having observed that your neighbour on the other side of the road is not experiencing the mishap, option **C** may seem to be a stupid thing to do, but be warned that electricity and water cuts are surprisingly localised in Turkey and it is a common occurrence that two sides of the same road are affected differently.

You can call the *kapıcı* or other tenants in the same block to make sure that it is nothing to do with your own electrical wiring system, that it is a local cut, but once this is confirmed, there is nothing you can do but bring out your candles and wait for the return of the power.

SITUATION SEVEN

On New Year's Eve you receive a beautiful watch from the managing director of a Turkish company, with his company card attached to it.

This puts you in an awkward position because you are negotiating with him for a business deal. You feel that if you accept the gift, you will have to accept his terms too, as if you have taken a bribe. On the other hand it may damage your business relationship with the company if you reject it. What should you do?

A. Accept the watch but make your business decisions regardless of it.

B. Return the watch, saying that it is against your ethics and your company policy to accept a gift of this value from a business contact.

C. Accept the watch and complete the deal in favour of the other company.

Comments

It is customary in the Turkish business world, especially that of Istanbul, to send impressive presents for the New Year. The items range from large boxes of Swiss chocolates to attractive hampers, from a selection of expensive drinks to exquisite Dior ties and cufflinks.

A watch received during this season falls within the same tradition and it is unnecessary to search for individualised motives in the act. Most probably a hundred other people have also received the same watch so the best course of action under the circumstances is still that described in option **A**.

A returned gift is likely to be taken as an insult and you should try to avoid this course of action.

SITUATION EIGHT

Just before your Christmas party, your downstairs neighbour tells you that his mother died the night before and apologises that he is unable to attend the party. What will you do?

A. Send him a bouquet of flowers with a sympathy card on it, and go on having the party as if nothing has happened.

B. Cancel the party.

C. Not cancel the party but tell all your guests to be extremely quiet throughout the occasion.

Comments

In Turkey people are very respectful to those who experience a death in the family.

In order to show their respect they avoid certain activities such as those involved in music and dance. On the night when you are having a party, the other neighbours will probably restrain themselves from even switching on their television or radio. So, not to be out of line, you might consider option **B** but in case this is not possible, then definitely **C**.

FURTHER READING

For Those Interested in History:

Bernard Lewis, *The Emergence of Modern Turkey*, OUP, 1968.

Lord Kinross, *Atatürk – The Rebirth of a Nation*, Weidenfeld and Nicolson, 1971

Roderic H. Davison, *Turkey*, Prentice Hall, 1968

Erik J. Zürcher, *Turkey: A Modern History*, I.B. Tauris & Co Ltd, 1993.

Philip Mansel, *Constantinople*, John Murray, 1995.

For People With Linguistic Interests:

G.L. Lewis, *Turkish Grammar*, OUP, 1967.

Arın Bayraktaroğlu and Sinan Bayraktaroğlu, *Colloquial Turkish*, Routledge, 1992.

For Literature Enthusiasts:

Talat S. Halman, *Contemporary Turkish Literature* (Fiction and Poetry), Associated University Presses Inc., 1982.

Nermin Menemencioglu, *The Penguin Book of Turkish Verse*, Penguin Books, 1978.

Latife Tekin, *Berji Kristin – Tales from the Garbage Hills*, Marion Boyars, 1993. A modern Turkish novelist describing life in the slums.

For Fine Arts and Archtecture Enthusiasts:

Henry Glassie (ed.), *Turkish Traditional Art Today*, Indiana University Press, 1993.

Godfrey Goodwin, *A History of Ottoman Architecture*, The John Hopkins Press, 1971.

Ekrem Akurgal, *The Art and Architecture of Turkey*, Oxford University Press, 1980.

Béla Bartok, *Turkish Folk Music from Asia Minor*, Princeton University Press, 1976.

For Tourists:

Dana Facaros and Michael Pauls, *Turkey*, Cadogan Books, 1986.

John Freely, *Blue Guide Istanbul*, W. Norton & Co., 1983.

Miscellaneous Reading:

Irfan Orga, *Portrait of a Turkish Family*, Eland Books, 1988. A very moving story of an Istanbul family from 1908 to 1970.

Kenize Mourad, *Farewell Princess*, Muller, 1990. The story of Princess Selma, the grand-daughter of Sultan Murad, in the last days of the Ottoman Empire and in exile.

Holly Chase, *Turkish Tapestry*, Bosphorus Books, 1993. Impressions of a most perceptive modern traveller in Turkey.

Shirin Devrim, *A Turkish Tapestry*, Quartet Books, 1994. The story of a well known family – the Shakirs of Istanbul. The resemblance of the title to Holly Chase's book is only a coincidence.

Raphaela Lewis, *Everyday Life in Ottoman Turkey*, Dorset Press, 1971. A classic on Ottoman life and culture.

THE AUTHOR

Dr Arın Bayraktaroğlu was Lector at the University of Cambridge 1977–1982 and is still involved with the university, teaching Turkish language and literature.

Since 1982 she has been Co-Director for The Cambridge Centre for Languages and Chief Examiner for the London University Board for the Advanced Level Turkish examinations. Her field of specialisation is ethnomethodology and conversation analysis.

As well as various publications in scientific journals, she has also published *Colloquial Turkish* (Routledge, 1992.) in collaboration with Sinan Bayraktaroğlu and translated the classic, *Portrait of a Turkish Family*.

She visits Turkey regularly and spends at least a month there every year.

ACKNOWLEDGEMENTS

I would like to thank Valerie Bevan, David Watkins and Dr Uygur Kocabasoğlu for reading and making comments on the text; Tan Oral for the illustrations; Izmir Tolga of Birlesik Reklamcılık A.S. in Turkey and the Turkish Tourist Office in London for the photographs and slides; Holly Chase for allowing me to quote from her work, and my husband, Sinan, for his encouragement and understanding during the preparation of this book.

INDEX